Bible Promises
for Women

Publications International, Ltd.

Contributing writer: Marie D. Jones

Cover and interior art: Shutterstock.com

Louis Weber, CEO
Publications International, Ltd.
8140 Lehigh Avenue
Morton Grove, Illinois 60053

Permission is never granted for commercial purposes.

ISBN: 978-1-68022-307-1

Manufactured in China.

8 7 6 5 4 3 2 1

Contents

The Promise of Today

The Bible is full of God's
promises. God promises to
love us forever. He promises
forgiveness. God promises
wisdom and instruction. He
promises his guidance and
encouragement for life. God
promises to bring comfort
and healing. He promises
to turn our mourning into
dancing and our weaknesses into strength.

The Apostle Peter wrote: "Whereby are given unto us
exceeding great and precious promises: that by these ye
might be partakers of the divine nature" (2 Peter 1:4). God's
promises are precious because they pertain to the most
meaningful and needful things of our lives. They are great
because they are beyond anything we could have hoped for

or imagined in their scope and power—and because, without fail, God will keep each one.

The Bible says God's ways are "unsearchable," far beyond our ability to fathom. But his promises reveal his true character. His promises show us that he is gracious and compassionate, full of mercy and truth. His promises show us that he is majestic and mysterious, filled with holy passion and power. Most of all, his promises show us that he is faithful, and has been faithful, not just to the patriarchs and the apostles, but to each of us, right down to this day.

Bible Promises for Women will help you discover many of these promises. Through scripture verses, prayers, and meditations, you will be reminded of God's steadfast love. You

 will consider the promise of his presence in everything from the mundane to the miraculous. You will find hope to strengthen your heart. You may even shout for joy—or at least hum a tune of thanksgiving. God's promises are not platitudes; they are powerful statements of who he is and what he does.

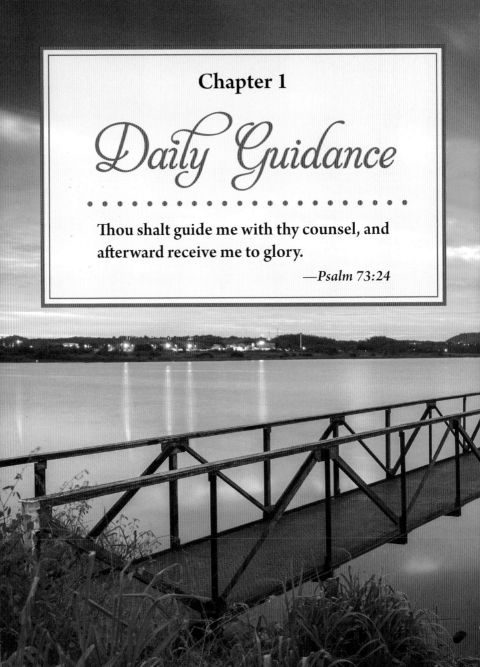

Chapter 1

Daily Guidance

Thou shalt guide me with thy counsel, and
afterward receive me to glory.

—*Psalm 73:24*

I exhort therefore, that, first of all,
supplications, prayers, intercessions, and giving of
thanks, be made for all men; For kings, and for all
that are in authority; that we may lead a quiet and
peaceable life in all godliness and honesty.

—1 Timothy 2:1–2

$\mathcal{L}$ife is full of trade-offs, Lord, and I need to make one.
Guide my search for a career where I can have both a
life and a living. Your balance is not found running in a
circle, but along a beckoning path where enough is more
than sufficient; where money comes second to family,
community, and self; where success takes on new
meaning; and where, in the giving up, I gain wealth
beyond belief.

Keep thy heart with all diligence;
for out of it are the issues of life.

—Proverbs 4:23

$\mathcal{G}$od, we live in a fast-moving time. There are so many
distractions. The very tools that help us navigate our days

can also unhinge us. How many times have I interrupted my husband as he shared a story in service to an incoming call or text? How many times have I multitasked admirably, taking advantage of all that the digital world allows, but in the process, neglected mindfulness—ignoring the flesh-and-blood people with whom I shared a room? It is impossible to be present and listen when I have one eye on my phone. God, please help me to retain my priorities, and to give the people I am with my full love and attention—my undivided self. May I always protect my heart and listen with my heart.

But the Lord said unto Samuel, Look not on his countenance, or on the height of his stature; because I have refused him: for the Lord seeth not as man seeth; for man looketh on the outward appearance, but the Lord looketh on the heart.

—1 Samuel 16:7

When teetering here on the "cutting edge" of technology, cyberspace, and everything in between, O God, it is reassuring to know that from the beginning of time, you guide, direct, and hear our voices as we continue to ask for guidance. Our scenery changes but you are eternal.

And the Lord said, I have pardoned according to
thy word: But as truly as I live, all the earth
shall be filled with the glory of the Lord.

—Numbers 14:20–21

ℒord, the best way I know to say thank you for your
wonderful guidance is to try to be the kind of person you
have taught me to be. Please continue to lift me up every
day as I strive to be my best self.

If we live in the Spirit, let us also walk in the Spirit.

—Galatians 5:25

𝒯hank you, Father, for your Holy Spirit, my guide
through each day. May I willingly follow, no matter
when or where. Help me to obey quickly when you
direct me to serve or forgive others. May I always be
thankful and rejoice in the blessings you point out to
me along the way.

Then shall the King say unto them
on his right hand, Come, ye blessed of my Father,
inherit the kingdom prepared for you
from the foundation of the world.

—*Matthew 25:34*

𝓘 wonder who I will be today. Will I be the woman, the individual spirit with individual hopes and dreams? Will I be the loving and supportive wife? Maybe I'll be called upon to be the good friend, the one who listens and offers sage advice. Will I be the perfect employee, who gets the job done right and on time? I imagine I will also

have to be the mother, who cleans up after and prods along and scolds and loves and forgives. Then again, it will probably be a day just like any other, when I will be called upon to be all these things and more. Lord, no matter what this day brings, help me get through it with your loving guidance.

I am the good shepherd, and know my sheep,
and am known of mine.

—*John 10:14*

*Y*our Word says—and I've heard it elsewhere—that a flock of sheep knows its own shepherd's voice and won't respond to the voice of a different shepherd. It's true of my relationship with you, too, Lord. I know your voice. I know when you're speaking to my heart, and I know when I'm being coaxed by "other voices"— wrong desires, worldly values, anxiety, pride, and the like. Thanks for helping me see the difference. Coax me to follow the sound of your voice today and always.

Blessed is the man that endureth temptation:
for when he is tried, he shall receive the crown of life,
which the Lord hath promised to them that love him.

—*James 1:12*

To spend my life with God is a choice I freely make. To love God and let God love me is the light of my life— what enables me to choose wisely and be thoughtful to those around me. God empowers me to resist temptation in the same breath that he compels me to give generously of my resources and myself. The blessing that James promises feels to me like God's love: It shines on me every day, lights the darkness, and illuminates my path.

Wherefore take unto you the whole armour of God,
that ye may be able to withstand in the evil day, and
having done all, to stand.

—*Ephesians 6:13*

Lord, be my warrior, my guard, and my guide. Let your love be the armor that shields me from the slings and arrows of the day. Let your compassion be the blanket that protects me from the cold at night. Lord, be my warrior, my champion, and my protector. Let your love surround me like an impenetrable light that nothing can break through to do me harm. Let your grace bring me peace no matter how crazy things are all around me. Lord, be my warrior.

And now the Lord shew kindness and truth unto you: and I also will requite you this kindness, because ye have done this thing.

—*2 Samuel 2:6*

It's hard to be pleasant these rude, road-raging days. Everyone's too immersed in their own concerns to be mannerly or kind. Encourage me to get in the first words of "please," "thanks," and "excuse me." Nudge me to be the first to take turns on the road, in the store, and at work. Maybe good manners will be as catching as rude ones. May I, with your guidance, be first to pass them on.

And they that be wise shall shine as the brightness
of the firmament; and they that turn many
to righteousness as the stars for ever and ever.

—*Daniel 12:3*

𝓛et me do what lies clearly at hand, this very minute. Grant me the insight to see that too much planning for the future removes me from the present moment. And this is the only existence, the only calling I have been given—right now to do what is necessary. Nothing more, nothing less. Thus may I use this next moment wisely.

And let it be, when these signs are come unto thee,
that thou do as occasion serve thee;
for God is with thee.

—*1 Samuel 10:7*

To those scanning a night sky, you sent a star. To those tending sheep on a silent hill, you sent a voice. What sign, Lord, are you sending me to come, be, and do all you intend? Let me hear, see, and accept it when you do.

Thou hast heard my voice: hide not thine ear
at my breathing, at my cry.

—*Lamentations 3:56*

Today, heavenly Father, you may call upon me to listen to someone and hear that person's heart. It may be someone who needs to feel significant enough to be heard, or perhaps someone who is lonely and longs to be connected to another person, or maybe someone who is hurting and needs a sympathetic ear. Whatever the case, Lord, please open my ears so that I may listen to someone today.

*Therefore I esteem all thy precepts concerning
all things to be right; and I hate every false way.*

—*Psalm 119:128*

*L*ord, teach me to think ahead about the results my
actions might inflict. If things go awry despite my
forethought, help me admit my wrongs and right them.

*For the word of God is quick, and powerful,
and sharper than any twoedged sword, piercing
even to the dividing asunder of soul and spirit,
and of the joints and marrow, and is a discerner
of the thoughts and intents of the heart.*

—*Hebrews 4:12*

*T*his morning I made coffee, checked my phone,
signed a permission slip, opened a novel. I dropped the
kids at school, checked Facebook, skimmed the news,
and answered emails—all this before starting my
workday. Is it any surprise that with the morning not
even behind me, I felt anxious and scattered? Lord,
my life is filled with so much information to sense and

absorb. Please help me to quiet my mind so that I may receive you; your Word pierces the distractions to challenge and bolster my heart.

Blessed are the pure in heart:
for they shall see God.

—Matthew 5:8

*H*ow can I be pure in heart, Lord? I certainly don't always have the right thoughts and motives. Perhaps being pure in heart can happen through being honest about what's going on inside my heart and working to purify it. I can make it a point to focus on what is right and true and good, continually turning my heart toward you to find those things and be renewed in them. That's why I'm here right now, Lord. Purify my heart as I walk close to you today and enjoy the blessing of fellowship with you.

Favour is deceitful, and beauty is vain:
but a woman that feareth the Lord,
she shall be praised.

—*Proverbs 31:30*

I dreamed as a young girl of growing up to be a beautiful princess living in a lavish castle with a handsome prince. But with age and wisdom came the realization that external beauty and favor isn't all it's cracked up to be. Today, I still care about my appearance, but minus the vanity of youth. Now I am much more focused on the beauty and strength that

comes from within. God, help me to build my inner beauty and let it shine out into the world. Instill in me courage and resilience and a spirit of love and compassion, because the world needs more love and compassion. Guide me to be a vessel of your bountiful blessings, God. May I always be beautiful in your eyes.

In all thy ways acknowledge him,
and he shall direct thy paths.

—*Proverbs 3:6*

ℰach day, I face dozens of decisions, big and small. The small ones are usually easy, like what to defrost for dinner, or which PJs I want to wear to bed. The bigger ones are not quite as easy, especially when they involve outcomes that directly affect my family or friends. I must remind myself throughout the day to stop and think— what would God want me to do? God's will is always the

right decision, even if it isn't the one I might have chosen. I can honestly say on several occasions, my own stubbornness and limited perception made problems worse, not better. God, I ask that you always direct my choices and guide my thoughts. I ask that your ways become my ways in everything I do.

But why dost thou judge thy brother?
or why dost thou set at nought thy brother?
for we shall all stand before the
judgment seat of Christ.

—*Romans 14:10*

When I am on Facebook or other social networking sites, I start to feel depressed. So much negativity, and so much judgment between people! Yet we are told not to judge others, because we will then be judged in return. God is the only judge there is; yet I see so many people playing judge, jury, and executioner for the sins and

mistakes of others. God, help us all to remember that judging is itself a sin, because it comes from pride and ego, and not from love and compassion. Help us, God, to open our hearts to those who stumble—not humiliate them. Help us remember that one day we are all going to stand in judgment to you, God, the only judge that matters.

Dearly beloved, avenge not yourselves,
but rather give place unto wrath:
for it is written, Vengeance is mine;
I will repay, saith the Lord.

—*Romans 12:19*

If someone sins against me, my first instinct is to find a way to punish him or her. I forget God's role is to judge, and mine is to forgive. It doesn't mean I condone what they did, but that I am letting go of the anger and resentment and letting God be the one to decide their fate. I am responsible for my own behavior, and as long as I stay centered in God's teachings and will, I sin less, and forgive more. God, I pray to have the patience and tolerance to step aside when someone steps on my toes, and let you deal with them accordingly. I pray for compassion and forgiveness, too, because compassion and forgiveness are what I would want from another if I were to sin against them.

Pride goeth before destruction, and an haughty spirit before a fall.

—Proverbs 16:18

$\mathcal{D}$o I have the right to be proud of my achievements? I've worked hard for them and they do make me feel accomplished and fulfilled. God asks that we not be too proud, and that we don't fall prey to vanity and bragging, for those are of the ego, and not of the spirit. I can be proud of my children, but know that God is at work through me raising them. I can take pride in my job, but understand God is there, too, flowing through me when I

am creative and efficient. God, help me find that balance between feeling good about my goals and not boasting and bragging to make myself feel better than others. Help me remember your role in all of my successes as the Manager and CEO of my life.

Wait on the Lord: be of good courage, and he shall strengthen thine heart: wait, I say, on the Lord.

—*Psalm 27:14*

God, I am scurrying around like a chicken with its head cut off, making a huge mess everywhere I go. Why, God, when I know I do better and work more efficiently when I wait quietly and listen for your guidance, do I rush about—driven by time rather than by you? Help me, God, to slow down, to be silent, so I can hear you and do your will, not mine.

To every thing there is a season,
and a time to every purpose under the heaven.

—*Ecclesiastes 3:1*

$\mathcal{D}$ear God, I thank you for the opportunity to do both of the things I love: being a mother and holding down a meaningful job. It has been hectic, Lord, and sometimes I wonder if my job is worth the late nights and weekends spent doing laundry and housework. I become so tired I can barely function.

I need your steadying hand, Father. I need you to help me discern what I can and cannot do. I need you to make the pieces fit. You help me find balance in my day—to find a time for every purpose. After school and evenings are for my kids and husband; late nights and Saturdays are for chores. I wait for Sundays, Lord, to be with you and renew myself in worship. I could not accomplish anything without your sweet spirit blowing through me, refreshing and strengthening me each day so I can give my best to my family and my job.

Wherefore we receiving a kingdom which cannot be moved, let us have grace, whereby we may serve God acceptably with reverence and godly fear.

—*Hebrews 12:28*

Who has time nowadays for the miracles of God's grace? Our lives are crammed with activities and obligations. We have family and friends to spend time with, and goals to accomplish. I cannot remember the last time I slowed down long enough to ask God his will for my life, can you? But without God's input, we usually end up spinning our wheels and feeling emptied and exhausted. We overburden and over-obligate ourselves. We push and force and control every aspect of our lives. God, I pray for more grace in my life, and in the lives of those I love. May I find that still place within where I can hear your voice directing me. May I learn to let you take control.

For when God made promise to Abraham, because
he could swear by no greater, he sware by himself,
Saying, Surely blessing I will bless thee,
and multiplying I will multiply thee. And so, after he
had patiently endured, he obtained the promise.

—*Hebrews 6:13–15*

*L*ord, my kids sometimes do the dumbest things,
skirting disaster. And while it's not possible to put an
old head on young shoulders, O God, I would if I could.
Help me find ways that will protect my impetuous young
ones without alienating them. Help me remember that
they are the greatest blessing.

O Lord, thou art my God; I will exalt thee, I will
praise thy name; for thou hast done wonderful
things; thy counsels of old are faithfulness and truth.

—*Isaiah 25:1*

I've been told a few times to get out of my own way.
It's true I am often my own worst enemy, especially when
it comes to making decisions. I waffle back and forth,

and usually end up not deciding and letting things just happen, which doesn't always work in my favor. I seem to forget if I put my faith and trust in God, and thank him for his presence, the answers I need miraculously appear. When I get out of my way and allow God his way, life works so much better and things go much smoother. God, if I am blocking

your light from reaching my heart, move me aside and take over. Your way is always the right way!

For as many as are led by the Spirit of God,
they are the sons of God.

—*Romans 8:14*

$\mathscr{E}$ncourage your child to learn, to master, to question— to try. It may feel like a big adventure and maybe even a huge risk, but you can relax, knowing that God is blessing the undertaking and providing the fuel for the journey.

*Hear thou, my son, and be wise, and
guide thine heart in the way.*

—*Proverbs 23:19*

God, I'm on such a roll. My children are doing well in school and activities; they're getting along with each other and acting like gracious, grown-up people. Maybe I'll change my mind a week from now but these moments are a great triumph. We parents do the hard daily work of teaching our children what's right and wrong, but the lessons all come from you, Lord, our guiding light. Thank you for this glimpse of the wonderful someday-adults we're hoping and working to raise together.

Stand fast therefore in the liberty wherewith
Christ hath made us free, and be not entangled
again with the yoke of bondage.

—Galatians 5:1

I love the freedoms I enjoy as your child, Father. I also deeply appreciate the freedoms I enjoy as a citizen of a free country. Both citizenships—my heavenly one and my earthly one—call for responsible living on my part, but these responsibilities are really a joy and a privilege. Help me to always keep this in the forefront of my mind as I make choices each day.

Delight thyself also in the Lord;
and he shall give thee the desires of thine heart.

—Psalm 37:4

E ver notice how thinking about what you are grateful for often leads to more things to be grateful for? When our hearts and eyes are focused on the amazing good God has given us, we realize we have little need for anything else. And yet...he gives us more. We can go to God in prayer and he answers, giving us the deepest yearnings of our hearts. It all starts with turning to God in the first place, and not to the ways and things of the world. If we start with God, we end up with all we have ever hoped for. Thank you, God, for fulfilling my deepest desires with your everlasting presence and love. Thank you for knowing my heart even better than I know it myself.

Let us do good unto all men, especially unto them who are of the household of faith.

—Galatians 6:10

𝒥f you were like me, you hated having your mom tell you to share your toys with your siblings. As kids, we want what is ours and don't like to share. Many of us grow up with that same fear of losing what we have if we show a little courtesy or kindness. God not only wants us to share, he multiplies our blessings when we do. When we give freely of what we have to struggling friends, family, and even strangers, our reward is the joy of serving others. But God also rewards us with even more to give. It's one of his most amazing miracles. Give, and more will be provided. Thank you, God, for your circle of abundant blessings.

I will extol thee, O Lord; for thou hast lifted me up,
and hast not made my foes to rejoice over me.

—*Psalm 30:1*

God, when life feels like a ride that won't let us off, remind us that you are waiting for us to reach up to you. And when we finally do, thank you for being there to lift us to peace and safety.

Chapter 2

Everyday Faith

• •

For we walk by faith, not by sight.
—*2 Corinthians 5:7*

Then shall we know, if we follow on to know the Lord:
his going forth is prepared as the morning;
and he shall come unto us as the rain,
as the latter and former rain unto the earth.

—Hosea 6:3

*H*ow certain the seasons are, Lord! How faithfully you usher them in one after the other, each in its assigned order. The spring has come with its rains once again, just as I knew it would. And spring's arrival reminds me that you—the faithful creator—have promised to dwell with those who long to know you, those who search for you and look for your return.

Wherefore, if God so clothe the grass of the field,
which to day is, and to morrow is cast into the oven,
shall not he much more clothe you, O ye of little faith?

—*Matthew 6:30*

I am so tired of worrying, God, about how to pay the bills, how to keep the kids safe, how to keep my friendships and marriage healthy. I feel so defeated at times, when it appears that the dark is overwhelming the light, and evil is so prevalent over good. Help me, God. Help me to refocus and relax in my faith and to remember that things are not always as they seem. Help me to remember all the ways you have come through for me. Help me to stand taller in faith instead of shrinking in fear before the ways of the world. Help restore my faith, God.

The Lord will perfect that which concerneth me:
thy mercy, O Lord, endureth for ever:
forsake not the works of thine own hands.

—*Psalm 138:8*

Lord, if there is one thing I can use more of, it's faith. Good, strong, solid faith. Faith in the harmony and order of a world I can't comprehend. Faith in the goodness of a society I often distrust. Faith that my family will be protected and loved, even when I'm not there to protect and love them. Most of all, dear Lord, I need faith in myself and in my abilities to grow as a woman, a wife, and a mother. So don't give me diamonds or fancy cars. Those I can do without. Give me faith. Good, strong, solid faith.

Faith is the substance of things hoped for,
the evidence of things not seen.

—*Hebrews 11:1*

*H*eavenly Father, what do I have to fear when you are the one caring for me? And yet, I do fear. Irrationally I fear, despite your faithfulness, despite your assurances, and despite your promises. Why do I still fear? I don't always understand my trembling heart and the shadows of things far smaller than you before which it cowers. Please liberate me from these lapses of trust. Free me to stand fearlessly, supported by faith and hope, in the center of your great love for me.

Trust in the Lord with all thine heart;
and lean not unto thine own understanding.

—*Proverbs 3:5*

Sometimes I work so hard to control everything that I need to be reminded to have faith and "let go." Last night my head was in a whirl: I lay in bed and stared into the darkness, worrying about bills, my workload, and if my husband and I would have time to care for the yard before the frost. My mind churned as I envisioned schemes, schedules, emails I might write, and ways to exert control. It was only when I "let go" and decided to give my concerns over to you that I gained some measure of peace, and was able to sleep. Lord, thank you for your support and guidance as I navigate my busy days. May I have the faith to trust you over my own understanding.

Thy faithfulness is unto all generations:
thou hast established the earth, and it abideth.

—*Psalm 119:90*

*H*uman faith lives between two extremes, Lord: It's neither completely blind nor able to see everything. It has plenty of evidence when it steps out and trusts you, but it takes each step with a good many questions still unanswered. It's quite an adventure, this life of faith. Lord, I must confess that experiencing your faithfulness over time makes it easier to trust you with the unknown in life. Thank you for your unshakable devotion.

Therefore I say unto you,
Take no thought for your life,
what ye shall eat, or what ye shall drink;
nor yet for your body, what ye shall put on.
Is not the life more than meat,
and the body than raiment?

—*Matthew 6:25*

Loving God, I confess that I worry too much. I worry about the welfare of my children. I worry about my husband's job. I worry about our budget, which buckles under the weight of our growing family. I even worry about worrying!

Forgive my doubts, my lack of faith and trust in you, O Lord. Teach me to express my family's needs to you daily in prayer and to trust in your ability to supply them.

In my heart, I know you will never let us down. With you in charge of our lives, we will want for nothing, for you take care of all your creations.

And Jesus said unto them, Because of your unbelief:
for verily I say unto you, If ye have faith as a grain of
mustard seed, ye shall say unto this mountain,
Remove hence to yonder place; and it shall remove;
and nothing shall be impossible unto you.

—*Matthew 17:20*

$\mathcal{I}$nto the bleakest winters of our souls, Lord, you are tiptoeing on tiny infant feet to find us. May we drop whatever we're doing and accept this gesture of a baby so small it may be overlooked in our frantic search for something massive and overwhelming. Remind us that it is not you who demands lavish celebrations and strobe-lit displays of faith. Rather, you ask only that we have the faith of a mustard seed and willingness to let a small hand take ours. We are ready.

Jesus said unto her, I am the resurrection,
and the life: he that believeth in me,
though he were dead, yet shall he live:
And whosoever liveth and believeth in me
shall never die. Believest thou this?

—*John 11:25–26*

*L*ord, I do believe in your promise of everlasting life! And because of my hope of life with you in eternity, there is all the more meaning for life today. There's meaning in my choices, my relationships, my work, my play, my worship. It all matters, it all counts, and I live knowing one day I'll stand in your presence with great joy.

And he changeth the times and the seasons:
he removeth kings, and setteth up kings:
he giveth wisdom unto the wise,
and knowledge to them that know understanding.

—*Daniel 2:21*

*W*e respond to stresses in our lives with either fear or faith. Fear is a great threat to our faith. That's why we read often in the scriptures the directive, "Fear not." The closer we draw to God, the more our fears diminish.

But let him ask in faith, nothing wavering.
For he that wavereth is like a wave
of the sea driven with the wind and tossed.

—*James 1:6*

God, it is hard to have faith all the time these days, especially when I lost my job. Money is tight and I don't know how I am going to support my family. I know that your ways are much higher than mine, and your plan for me is one I cannot imagine, but I need help during these

dark times to keep my solid foundation of faith intact. My children depend on me and look up to me as a model of a strong and faithful woman. Show me how, dear God, I can be the best role model for my kids. Help me solidify my own faith, so that I can be the best mom and person I can be.

*Let us draw near with a true heart in
full assurance of faith, having our hearts sprinkled
from an evil conscience, and our bodies
washed with pure water.*

—Hebrews 10:22

$\mathscr{F}$riendships end, and it can really hurt when someone decides they don't want to be a part of our lives anymore. We feel rejected, guilty, and broken. Truth is, people who don't want to be in our lives weren't meant to stay. This is when we must turn to God in faith and understand that

his plan for us may not include the people we think it should. God knows best whom we have outgrown. So when a friendship reaches the final bend in the road, trust that God is going to lead us around the corner to something, and someone, new. Be assured God knows who we should walk our path with, and when to let go and walk alone.

And Joshua said unto them, "Fear not,
nor be dismayed, be strong and of good courage:
for thus shall the Lord do to all your enemies
against whom ye fight."

—Joshua 10:25

God, teach me to not fear adversity. It is a mother's knee-jerk reaction to protect her children from all trials, but one cannot travel through life without reversals of fortune. Help me to accept and face challenges not only to myself but also to my children. My kids will face unkindness; they will  face unfairness, loss, and even cruelty in their life's journey. God, help me to remember that adversity breeds character—that we cannot necessarily control what happens to us but we can control our response to it. Grant me the strength to respond to adversity with grace, and please guide me as I give my children the tools to greet life's ups and downs with faith in you, and with courage.

Know therefore that the Lord thy God,
he is God, the faithful God,
which keepeth covenant and mercy with them
that love him and keep his commandments
to a thousand generations.

—Deuteronomy 7:9

We are creatures of habit with default settings that bring us back to anxiety and fear every time we are presented with a new obstacle or challenge. Isn't that the truth? I know I do that. I forget you have never abandoned me, God, and I sink into depression or worry at the drop of a hat. I know you are faithful to me, and unceasingly so. Why can't I be more unceasingly faithful to you? I aspire to know and experience more of your grace, and to be an example of a strong faithful person to my family. Forgive me for the times I forget you never turn away from me, God, even though I may turn away from you.

Fight the good fight of faith,
lay hold on eternal life,
whereunto thou art also called,
and hast professed a good profession
before many witnesses.

—1 Timothy 6:12

$\mathcal{I}$ wonder who can really have faith in good anymore with so much bad in the world. Seeing the death and destruction makes me question my own faith, God. I am sorry to admit that. This is when I most need to turn to you in prayer, God, and to ask not just for help coping, but help in recovering my faith. I know your ways are mysterious, and I cannot understand them, but please help me turn back to faith when fear threatens to overtake me. There is so much love and good out there,

God. Keep my eyes on the sun, and when darkness comes, keep my heart focused on your light to guide me through the night.

*By faith they passed through
the Red sea as by dry land: which the
Egyptians assaying to do were drowned.*

—*Hebrews 11:29*

*R*emember as a child how much instant faith we had in life? We believed in good and our spirits were wild and free. Lord, I thank you for reminding me that even now, as an adult, I can find that same instant faith, and that same free spirit by keeping your ways. My faith may not move mountains, but it's enough to move the mountains in my day-to-day life. My faith may not part oceans, but

it's enough to close great divides when my loved ones are fighting. My faith may not heal millions, but if I can use it to heal just one person, that is enough. Thank you, Lord, for the miracles big and small with which you've blessed my life.

And the Lord, he it is that doth go before thee;
he will be with thee, he will not fail thee,
neither forsake thee: fear not, neither be dismayed.

—*Deuteronomy 31:8*

*L*ord, give me the faith to take the next step, even when I don't know what lies head. Give me the assurance that even if I stumble and fall, you'll pick me up and put me back on the path. And give me the confidence that, even if I lose faith, you will never lose me.

For by grace are ye saved through faith;
and that not of yourselves: it is the gift of God:
Not of works, lest any man should boast.

—*Ephesians 2:8–9*

*L*ord, I am grateful that you don't have a list of criteria for being eligible for salvation. What insecurity that would create in me! I feel blessed that I don't need to resort to servile fear or self-important boasting when it comes to my standing with you. Your salvation is a gift available to all and secured by your merits, not mine. It is received only by grace through faith in you.

Above all, taking the shield of faith,
wherewith ye shall be able to quench
all the fiery darts of the wicked.

—Ephesians 6:16

Today I face a frightening health issue, God, and I am more afraid than I would like to admit. Nobody wants illness. Nobody wants to go under the knife or be told they may not live to see their children grow up. But I have you, God, and with your presence today, I know I can get through any challenge. I know I can stand up to the fear and the worry and vanquish it with love and faith. I know you don't give me more than I can handle, God, and that you'll be there to handle it with me nonetheless. Thank you, God, for being my shield and my rock and my faithful warrior.

And I say unto you, Ask, and it shall be given you;
seek, and ye shall find; knock, and it shall be opened
unto you. For every one that asketh receiveth;
and he that seeketh findeth;
and to him that knocketh it shall be opened.

—Luke 11:9–10

ℒord, I know you will show your goodness and faithfulness to me if I just diligently seek you. The problem isn't your willingness to give, but my tendency to try to do everything by myself rather than leaning on and trusting in you. This silly inclination brings me needless stress and wastes precious time. Today I endeavor to lay my needs and troubles at your feet the minute I begin to feel the least bit overwhelmed.

The wind bloweth where it listeth,
and thou hearest the sound thereof,
but canst not tell whence it cometh,
and whither it goeth:
so is every one that is born of the Spirit.

—John 3:8

When the winds of change and challenge blow hard into my life, I will take refuge in you, O Lord. When the darkness descends upon my home, I will fear not, for I will place my faith in you. When my child is ill or my husband is hurt, I will remain steadfast, for I know that you will be right there by my side, O Lord. Although I cannot see you, I know you are always with me, O Lord, and in that I take comfort and find strength.

There is therefore now no condemnation to them
which are in Christ Jesus, who walk
not after the flesh, but after the Spirit.
For the law of the Spirit of life in Christ Jesus
hath made me free from the law of sin and death.

—Romans 8:1–2

$\mathcal{L}$ord, how I long to stand strong in the faith! I read of the martyrs of old and question my own loyalty and courage. Would I, if my life hung in the balance, say, "Yes, I believe in God"? I pray I would, Lord. Continue to prepare me for any opportunity to stand firm for what I know to be true. To live without conviction is hardly to live at all.

So that we may boldly say, The Lord is my helper, and I will not fear what man shall do unto me.

—*Hebrews 13:6*

$\mathcal{M}$ay I have a moment to speak with you, O God? I know there is so much going on in the world that requires your attention. It's just that sometimes I feel tension getting a grip on me and worry clouds my view. This distances me from you and from everything in my life. I pray for the freedom to worry less. I want to simply trust you more.

But we are not of them who draw back unto perdition;
but of them that believe to the saving of the soul.

—*Hebrews 10:39*

We all know a "shrinking violet," someone who shies away from attention. But being a Christian means doing the opposite. Who made a bigger splash in history than Jesus Christ? It's important to stand confidently in your faith and embrace it with your whole heart. To shy away from the message or what it means in your life is to shirk God's teachings.

But without faith it is impossible to please him: for he
that cometh to God must believe that he is, and that he
is a rewarder of them that diligently seek him.

—*Hebrews 11:6*

Lord, I must deal with people who don't have any faith in you, in life, or in themselves. They whine and complain, and it saps my energy. They only believe in what they can see, and what they see is pain, fear, and worry. I know telling them to have faith won't help. So I ask that you use me as an example of how joyous and peaceful life can be when you do the driving. Let the rewards and blessings you've bestowed on me serve as a reminder of what having simple faith can do for someone who is lost, alone, and afraid.

Charge them that are rich in this world, that they be not highminded, nor trust in uncertain riches, but in the living God, who giveth us richly all things to enjoy.

—*1 Timothy 6:17*

I love when all my plans come to fruition, and money is rolling in, my loved ones are happy and healthy, and everything happens with ease and grace. Those times remind me that working hard and having faith do count in the eyes of God, who loves me and provides for me. But I never put all my faith in money and success. I've had them taken away just as quickly as I've earned them. Enjoy them? Yes. But lean on them? No. The only thing I lean on is the ever-present love of God, which never diminishes or decreases. Thank you, God, for being my one true provider.

Chapter 3

Family

· ·

For this cause I bow my knees unto the
Father of our Lord Jesus Christ, Of
whom the whole family in heaven and
earth is named, That he would grant you,
according to the riches of his glory, to
be strengthened with might by his Spirit
in the inner man.

—*Ephesians 3:14–16*

*And Ruth said, Intreat me not to leave thee, or to
return from following after thee: for whither thou
goest, I will go; and where thou lodgest, I will lodge:
thy people shall be my people, and thy God my God.*

—*Ruth 1:16*

Children have the most amazing capacity for loyalty,
God. They look to their parents with trust that all will be
well. Sometimes I fear that I cannot live up to the faith
that my children put in me, that I am not as strong or as
invincible as they believe me to be. Lord, help me
appreciate their trust as the privilege that it is. Help me
to be a rock for my young ones, even as you are a rock for
me. You see into my heart; you know the strength and
fear that exist side by side within it. May you guide me—
helping me access the strength I possess and the strength
you give freely—as I strive to create a stable and loving
home life for my family.

*Forbearing one another, and forgiving one another,
if any man have a quarrel against any:
even as Christ forgave you, so also do ye.*

—*Colossians 3:13*

$\mathcal{M}$y husband and I got into a silly quarrel, O God of peacemaking and love, and we are having a hard time making up. Please guide us to common ground where you hold each of us by the hand and inspire us toward compromise. Amen.

Because he laid down his life for us: and we ought to lay down our lives for the brethren. But whoso hath this world's good, and seeth his brother have need, and shutteth up his bowels of compassion from him, how dwelleth the love of God in him?

—*1 John 3:16–17*

$\mathcal{T}$he love and devotion of family serves as the foundation upon which faith is built. The support of family acts both as wings to fly and a safety net to catch us. The honesty and trustworthiness of family creates both sanctuary and accountability for each of us in our journeys.

Children, obey your parents in all things:
for this is well pleasing unto the Lord.

—*Colossians 3:20*

$\mathcal{D}$ear Lord, I am officially in the "Sandwich Generation," raising my own children while helping my parents navigate the challenges of aging. Dad has developed Parkinson's, and Mom's arthritis is getting worse. My husband and I are devoted to helping them with practical matters like getting to the doctor, cleaning their home,

and buying groceries, and I have recently started bringing my older daughter along when we run errands with Mom. The challenges my folks face make me keenly aware of life's cycles of loss and change. I know my daughter feels it, too. But my hope is that these dates with Mom might be a way to demonstrate to my daughter what respect for elders can mean. Aging is a part of being, and compassion is an important lesson. Dear God, help me set the right example for my children through my relationship with my own parents.

Beloved, if God so loved us,
we ought also to love one another.

—1 John 4:11

$\mathscr{L}$ord, we want to honor the grandparents who tended us
so well. Pause with us as we play again in the dusty lanes of
childhood at Grandma and Grandpa's house. Bless these
bigger-than-life companions who helped us bridge home
and away, childhood and maturity. Thank you for such a
heritage and an opportunity to express our gratitude.

Talk no more so exceeding proudly; let not arrogancy
come out of your mouth: for the Lord is a God of
knowledge, and by him actions are weighed.

—1 Samuel 2:3

$\mathscr{L}$ord, nothing is more humbling than the loved ones
who've known me my whole life. When I catch up with
my siblings and cousins, we are anchored by memories of
silly childhood choices and even serious adult mistakes.
I'm blessed to have people in my life with whom I share
so much history and so many special memories; people
who forgive me and see the whole person I am.

Ye shall not respect persons in judgment;
but ye shall hear the small as well as the great;
ye shall not be afraid of the face of man;
for the judgment is God's.

—Deuteronomy 1:17

Lord, today I slighted one of my children without meaning to. I didn't listen when he offered his opinion, and he wondered if I dismissed him as being "just a kid." Everyone is special and everyone has valid input to offer. It's my responsibility to raise my children to be confident, thoughtful people. My son forgave me with great poise—I am as proud of him as I am embarrassed for myself. Thank you, God, for the blessing of his sweet personality and growing presence of mind.

*"The Lord bless him!" Naomi said to her
daughter-in-law. "He has not stopped showing
his kindness to the living and the dead."
She added, "That man is our close relative;
he is one of our guardian-redeemers."*

—Ruth 2:20

We are all connected, Lord, and may I impress upon my children the importance of this fact. It is one thing to talk about our connection to all living things, but it is quite another to live it. Help me to demonstrate—not only in my words, but also my actions— the fundamental role loving-kindness should play in our

lives. Whether it is aid to an injured animal, support and a listening ear to one who grieves, or respectful words spoken about someone who is deceased, may I put good into the world without expectation of recognition or reward. May I do good simply for the sake of doing good, and may I never stop showing kindness to those in need.

Forsake her not, and she shall preserve thee:
love her, and she shall keep thee.

—*Proverbs 4:6*

Women are both simple and complex. Yes, we have our quirks and unique qualities. But on a deeper level, we just want to love and be loved. In relationships, we are often the diplomats, bringing a sense of balance and unity to everything we do. When we are loved and acknowledged by those we care about, we don't glow... we shine! We don't need fancy things to make us happy.

We need love—as mothers, wives, sisters, daughters, and friends. God, may I always give love to others, and receive it just as gracefully. May I be a representative of the love you've given me, spreading it to everyone I come in contact with. May I appreciate, and be appreciated. May I bless, and be blessed in return.

Judge not, that ye be not judged.

—*Matthew 7:1*

$\mathcal{D}$ear Lord, I have a daughter in middle school. She and her friends are coming into their own, trying to figure out who they are. Technology makes it even simpler to be unkind, and it is tempting to adopt a judgmental attitude in order to fit in with others. God, help me guide my children as they navigate this time of change and growth. Please protect my family from the ways of the judgmental, and from adopting those ways in their interactions with others.

Think not that I am come to destroy the law,
or the prophets: I am not come to destroy,
but to fulfill.

—Matthew 5:17

$\mathcal{D}$ear God, in my efforts to forge my own best path and be a role model, may I always respect those who raised children before me. May I not challenge convention simply for the sake of doing so, and may I always do so with respect and propriety. God, please keep me mindful of the example Jesus set: to respect the ways of his elders and ancestors. He did not come to destroy their ways but to uphold and better them.

And if one prevail against him,
two shall withstand him;
and a threefold cord is not quickly broken.

—Ecclesiastes 4:12

My husband and I don't attend church every Sunday, but each weekend we make time to read scripture and talk about the week, which we try to view through the lens of spirituality. A difficult coworker, good news in our extended families—we'll discuss the good and the bad and talk about how God informs each ebb and flow. Sometimes we'll share a joy, such as the time my husband built a new bird feeder and we both discovered the great calm and pleasure we derived from watching the sparrows and finches. I think we both gain a lot from these quiet, regular moments of sharing. The Bible reminds me how your presence in my life, and my husband's life, creates a powerful "threefold cord." God, if my marriage is grounded in you, it will be strong.

So we, being many, are one body in Christ,
and every one members one of another.

—Romans 12:5

Family is about more than those with which you share a blood lineage. I have close friends who are like family to me. I trust them and lean on them for support. I cheerlead for them and care for them, just as I would a member of my family. Christ reminds us to love everyone as he loves us. We are all family in the eyes of the Lord. Even someone we barely know today can become a close friend tomorrow. Lord, help me to embrace all of your beloved children as members of my own family. Help me to open my arms and my heart to those who don't share my last name, but share your name and the love and kinship we have for you. We are all your family, Lord.

For my brethren and companions' sakes,
I will now say, Peace be within thee.

—*Psalm 122:8*

$\mathcal{E}$nter and bless this family, Lord, so that its circle will be where quarrels are made up and relationships mature; where failures are forgiven and new directions found.

For this child I prayed; and the Lord hath given me
my petition which I asked of him:
Therefore also I have lent him to the Lord;
as long as he liveth he shall be lent to the Lord.
And he worshipped the Lord there.

—*1 Samuel 1:27–28*

$\mathcal{T}$hank you, loving God, for my mother with whom I share a connection to the children. It was her loving care and ceaseless attention that has empowered me to mother. I am humbled by her steadfastness. I am a much-blessed daughter.

And he arose, and came to his father.
But when he was yet a great way off,
his father saw him, and had compassion, and ran,
and fell on his neck, and kissed him.
And the son said unto him,
Father, I have sinned against heaven, and in thy sight,
and am no more worthy to be called thy son.

—*Luke 15:20–21*

I love the story of the prodigal son. It reminds me of the bond parents and children share, and it reminds me of the simple fact that our children are human. They are going to make mistakes; sometimes they are going to disappoint us, deeply. But as parents, we are called upon to love our children, and forgive them, even when they have hurt us. (God, I suppose you know exactly what I mean: Even when I make mistakes, your love for me remains a constant.) Dear Lord, may I have the strength and wisdom to always love my children and be there for them, even when they disobey.

Behold, what manner of love the Father hath
bestowed upon us, that we should be called the sons
of God: therefore the world knoweth us not,
because it knew him not.

—1 John 3:1

$\mathcal{L}$et your peace rest upon our home, dear God. We do not know how to love one another as you have loved us. We fail to reach out the way you have gathered us in. We forget how to give when only taking fills our minds. And, most of all, we need your presence to remind us we are more than just parents and children. We are always your beloved sons and daughters here. Let your peace rest upon our home, dear God.

Honour thy father and thy mother:
that thy days may be long upon the land
which the Lord thy God giveth thee.

—Exodus 20:12

$\mathcal{I}$ am guilty of not always telling my parents how much they've done for me. I take for granted that they already know. But now as a mom, I can say with certainty that a little appreciation goes a long way, and I am trying harder to tell my parents how much I love and appreciate them. When my own children acknowledge me and show me affection, I feel whole and complete. When they take a moment out of their busy lives to call or come for a visit, I am happy and fulfilled. Help me remember, God, to make my own parents feel loved and appreciated more often. Help me show them every chance I get just how much they mean to me.

He that spareth his rod hateth his son:
but he that loveth him chasteneth him betimes.

—*Proverbs 13:24*

My son doesn't like doing homework. It's hard for him—he struggles with academics and he'd rather be playing baseball, a sport at which he excels. God, I don't like conflict. And we can butt heads when I insist he complete his work before play: I have lost my temper on more than one occasion, frustrated because he needs to do the work and yet doesn't want to do the work. Frustrated because I don't like to fight with him.

Sometimes I am tired and tempted to just let it go, though I know this would do him no favors. Dear God, help me to step up to the plate and be the adult I need to be. Please give me the strength to discipline my children when necessary, and help me to do so with love.

But if any provide not for his own,
and specially for those of his own house,
he hath denied the faith, and is worse than an infidel.

—*1 Timothy 5:8*

As a woman, I have to work twice as hard to balance the needs of my family and my job. My income helps the household, so I cannot stop working. But the most important job to me is being a great mom and wife. I go to bed most nights exhausted and worn down trying to juggle both. God, I pray for the extra energy and strength needed to get done what needs to be done at work, with plenty left over for the ones who love and depend on me at home. I pray for balance in my life and the wisdom to know what to do when home and work are both tugging at me for my attention.

For I know the thoughts that I think toward you,
saith the Lord, thoughts of peace, and not of evil,
to give you an expected end.

—Jeremiah 29:11

*W*hen a long-term relationship ends, it's natural to mourn the loss of a companion and to grieve the death of a particular way of life. But we can only mourn and grieve for so long; then we must ask God to give us the grace and the courage to finally close that door and walk toward a new door waiting to be opened. We must take the next step God has for us.

The fear of the Lord is the beginning of knowledge:
but fools despise wisdom and instruction.

—*Proverbs 1:7*

God, my children are entering their teenage years, a time when they might think they know best and are immune to tutelage. How many times of late have they responded to my suggestions with impatience or even scorn? Help me to guide them with patience—to remind them, in love, of the importance of remaining open to instruction. May they keep your essence a grounding influence as they learn and grow, and may I remember that I, too, must always remain open to what you and the world have to teach me. We are never "done," are we? Lord, help me to keep my love of God at the center of my journey of learning and teach my children to do the same.

And Jesus said unto them, I am the bread of life:
he that cometh to me shall never hunger;
and he that believeth on me shall never thirst.

—John 6:35

God of providence, as I work to satisfy the hunger and thirst of my husband and child, I can feel your presence here in my kitchen, directing me and loving me. I remember with a thankful heart that you feed my family, too. I may appease their physical hunger, but you satisfy their hungry hearts with heavenly food—"the Bread of Life"—your son, Jesus Christ.

O God, who each day gives us our daily bread, bless my kitchen today as I use it to prepare nourishment for my family. My heart overflows as I joyfully cook and serve the meals in an act of love and worship.

And above all things have fervent charity among yourselves: for charity shall cover the multitude of sins.

—1 Peter 4:8

My husband and I are newly married, and we encounter some growing pains as we adjust to sharing a home and a life together. One persistent source of discord is the fact that I am something of a neatnik, while my husband is more relaxed about keeping our apartment tidy. I can see that he tries, but it still drives me a little crazy when he leaves

dirty dishes on the counter, or toothpaste spatters in the sink. These are such little things, but sometimes they get to me, and I said as much to my mother the last time we were together. She responded to me with gentle humor: "Choose your battles and remember: love helps us overlook one another's flaws." My parents have an extraordinarily loving marriage, and Mom's words have stayed with me. Dear Lord, please help me remember that love is the root of a strong marriage, and that love helps us accept our partners as they are, warts and all.

And this commandment have we from him,
That he who loveth God love his brother also.

—*1 John 4:21*

𝓛ord, look down upon my family with merciful eyes, and help us to heal the divides that threaten to grow between us. Guide us toward the solutions that will empower everyone involved, and remind us that we work better when we work together. Help us to speak honestly with each other. Amen.

And, ye fathers, provoke not your children to wrath:
but bring them up in the nurture and admonition
of the Lord.

—Ephesians 6:4

When it comes to my family, I've found that nurturing with a firm hand works wonders over anger and punishment. Sure, there are times I get mad and have to lay down the law, but I aspire to do so with love and compassion, as the Lord would admonish me if I were to sin. As a woman, I am a built-in nurturing machine. Balancing my need to be nurturing with my need to also provide structure and rules is a challenge. I look to you, Lord, for that proper balance. Through your wise and caring guidance, Lord, may I find just the right things to do and say.

And whether one member suffer, all the members suffer with it; or one member be honoured, all the members rejoice with it.

—*1 Corinthians 12:26*

The bond of family means that I cry and feel pain when my loved ones do, and I celebrate and rejoice with them, too. We are connected in heart, mind, and spirit in such a way that what harms one, harms all, and what makes one of us happy spreads happiness throughout the entire family. God is the glue that binds us together. Our shared love for each other and for God keeps us strong and united in good times and bad. I am so grateful, God, for my family and the amazing bond we share. I am grateful for these wonderful people to call my own, God, even as we are all a part of your beloved family.

*Therefore shall a man leave his father and his
mother, and shall cleave unto his wife:
and they shall be one flesh.*

—*Genesis 2:24*

$\mathscr{L}$ove is a challenge. Marriage is an even bigger one. Being a good wife often means compromising with my spouse and finding the balance in our relationship. I can get selfish and want what I want, but a true partnership strives to satisfy the needs of both, not just one. Marriage often means thinking in terms of the unit, not just the individuals. God, may you always be present in my marriage, guiding me and encouraging me to be the best wife I can be to my husband. I ask you, God, to empower me with the wisdom, patience, and understanding that makes a partnership a happy one for both parties involved. May I always focus on the bigger unit we chose when we said, "I do."

*Moreover if thy brother shall trespass against thee,
go and tell him his fault between thee and him alone:
if he shall hear thee, thou hast gained thy brother.*

—*Matthew 18:15*

$\mathcal{I}$ cannot stand fighting with family members. But it happens, and being hurt by someone so close leaves scars. If I keep resentment in my heart, it keeps me in an unloving place where even God cannot work through me. I think communication is key, and also being willing to forgive. I've found that when I talk to the person alone, without anger or judgment, we can usually work out any problem. God, may I always approach family conflicts with love, compassion, and forgiveness in my heart. I am not perfect, and shouldn't expect my family to be. God, may I always be willing to make amends to those I harm, and forgive those who harm me.

Chapter 4

Forgiveness

· ·

Be ye angry, and sin not: let not the sun go down upon your wrath: Neither give place to the devil.

—Ephesians 4:26–27

*H*eavenly Father, teach me to forgive others their transgressions and to let go of angers and resentments that poison the heart and burden the soul. Teach me to love and understand others and to accept them as they are, not as I wish they would be. Amen.

As far as the east is from the west,
so far hath he removed our transgressions from us.

—Psalm 103:12

$\mathcal{O}$ Lord, when you promise us you have removed our sins from us, why do we dredge them up so we can wallow in regret and shame all over again? Keep us from wasting time and energy thinking about past mistakes, Lord. If they are no longer on your radar, they surely don't belong on ours. How blessed we are to have such a compassionate, forgiving God!

Behold, I send an Angel before thee,
to keep thee in the way, and to bring thee
into the place which I have prepared.

—Exodus 23:20

$\mathcal{L}$ord, your forgiveness, based on your love for me, has transformed my life. I've experienced inner healing and freedom in knowing that you have wiped my slate clean and made me your friend. Help me to become an extension of your love to those around me. Let healing happen as

I apply the salve to the wounds they inflict on me. Please strengthen me while I carry it out in your name.

A soft answer turneth away wrath:
but grievous words stir up anger.

—*Proverbs 15:1*

Friends fight. Spouses fight. Parents and children fight. It happens, but when I fight back with angry and harsh words, I live to regret it. I recall many times saying things I didn't mean in the heat of the moment. Words hurt, and the wounds can stick around for a long time. Guide me, God, to pick my words carefully and respond with as much compassion as possible. If the situation is too volatile, help me to walk away until I am calm and operating from love, not hatred or rage or bitterness. Those are the times I most need you there, God, to remind me that what I say to another person can either help or harm them. Help me, God, to choose to help them every time.

Wherefore I say unto thee, Her sins,
which are many, are forgiven; for she loved much:
but to whom little is forgiven, the same loveth little.

—*Luke 7:47*

$\mathcal{L}$ord, it is tempting and easy to cast a scornful eye on those around us and note every fault. When my pride tempts me to do so, prompt me to turn the magnifying glass on myself instead. If I keep in mind how much I need your forgiveness every day, my love for you will never grow cold. I know you are willing to forgive each and every fault if I only ask.

I have blotted out, as a thick cloud, thy transgressions,
and, as a cloud, thy sins: return unto me;
for I have redeemed thee.

—Isaiah 44:22

Tossing leaves onto a fire, we name them as regrets and failures from which we choose to be free. We trust you to redeem even these, our deadest moments. They, like autumn leaves, can make the brightest blaze.

Stir new possibilities into life from the embers; fan the sparks of dreams so that we may become one with your purpose for us. It is the root from which we—leaf and human life—begin and from which the most amazing new creation can burst into being, a flame in the darkness.

Judge not, and ye shall not be judged:
condemn not, and ye shall not be condemned:
forgive, and ye shall be forgiven.

—*Luke 6:37*

Forgiveness includes letting go of the little things. Keeping a growing account of the small misdeeds of others in our memory bank is a formula for relational bankruptcy. Accumulating offenses, rather than forgiving them, feeds resentment and anger, and it chokes out our ability to love. "Forbearing one another, and forgiving one another" Paul taught; "even as Christ forgave you, so also do ye" (Colossians 3:13). Choosing to forgive people—even for the littlest things they do that hurt or annoy us—is vital for enjoying life and love.

Fret not thyself because of evildoers, neither be thou envious against the workers of iniquity. For they shall soon be cut down like the grass, and wither as the green herb. Commit thy way unto the Lord; trust also in him; and he shall bring it to pass.

—*Psalm 37:1–2, 5*

*P*lease, Lord, step into this situation. I don't know what to do. Things were done, words were said, and now I'm at odds with someone. Maybe I was wrong, but I don't think so. Honestly, I want to blame the other person for all of it, but maybe I have a blind spot. I want to sort things out and turn things around, but I'm not sure where to start. I don't know if a half-baked apology will do any good, especially if I don't really mean it.

And actually, I should be receiving an apology, but I doubt that will ever happen. I beg you, please do your work here. Shine your light so we see things clearly. Use your power to dismantle whatever grudges we have piled up. I commit this whole mess to you.

In whom we have redemption through his blood,
the forgiveness of sins,
according to the riches of his grace.

—Ephesians 1:7

What does redemption mean? To me, it means to be cleansed and renewed, free from the burdens of my past mistakes. God, your forgiveness brings me that clarity and redemption, and that renewal of my spirit. Your grace frees me from the bonds of the past that weighed me down and made my life feel so heavy. I ask in prayer today that you work with me to free those who I've kept in the bondage of their sins against me. Help me forgive them, not just because it will set me free of anger and pain in the process, but also because you have already forgiven them. We all sin. We all deserve to be made clean and whole again.

He that covereth a transgression seeketh love;
but he that repeateth a matter
separateth very friends.

—*Proverbs 17:9*

No matter how hard I try, God of patience and support, someone finds fault with me. I am mortified about the latest criticism. I can't decide whether to run away in shame or storm back and defend my actions, for I thought I was right. Criticism hurts most when coupled with ridicule, and I feel like less of a person for the tone in which I was addressed. Give me the courage to confront this, Lord, for it is not acceptable to be treated this way even when in error. Keep me calm, factual, and open; perhaps the tone was unintentional, the critic unaware of the power of shaming. Help me remember how I feel now the next time I find fault with someone. As I've learned firsthand with you the zillions of times I messed up, there are better ways to confront mistakes than with stinging criticisms that divide and demean. Truth be known, Lord, such abrasive manners say more about the criticizer than the criticized. Keep me from passing them on.

And when ye stand praying, forgive, if ye have ought against any: that your Father also which is in heaven may forgive you your trespasses.

—*Mark 11:25*

𝒻ather, I need to understand that forgiveness is not dependent on my feelings, but rather on a determination of my will. Help me form a few well-chosen words of forgiveness. Amen.

And forgive us our debts, as we forgive our debtors.

—*Matthew 6:12*

ℒord God, the words "I'm sorry" and "forgive me" have got to be the most powerful in our vocabulary. May these phrases ever be poised on my lips, ready to do their work of release and restoration. Let your healing balm wash over me, as I both grant and receive the freedom that forgiveness brings.

*So that contrariwise ye ought rather to forgive him,
and comfort him, lest perhaps such a one should be
swallowed up with overmuch sorrow.*

—*2 Corinthians 2:7*

Heavenly Father, when we stand to cross the
metaphorical bridge of forgiveness, please give us a
little push to get us going. Amen.

Thus saith the Lord of hosts; Consider your ways.

—*Haggai 1:7*

Gently, Lord, love me gently on this tough day. I'm hurting now because of my own mistake. It's nothing serious, but it especially hurts to know I brought the pain upon myself and disappointed you. The silver lining is that I know how to resolve the situation. Lord, I love that your Word and my own feelings coincide when it comes to knowing right from wrong, even if I sometimes ignore my better judgment. Thank you for welcoming me back into the fold every time without fail.

Confess your faults one to another,
and pray one for another, that ye may be healed.
The effectual fervent prayer
of a righteous man availeth much.

—James 5:16

In the past, I could never imagine my own faults made me responsible for my problems. Me? No, it had to be others who were at fault! Lord, you shook up my ego and made me see this was an excuse for giving up responsibility and power so I could play the victim and blame others, rather than look in the mirror and see my

own brokenness. Now I own up to my mistakes, ask through amends for forgiveness, and pray for others just as much as for myself. Happiness and wholeness isn't about getting my needs met at the expense of others. It's about recognizing where I've gone astray, and letting you lead me home again. Thank you, Lord.

For if ye forgive men their trespasses,
your heavenly Father will also forgive you.

—*Matthew 6:14*

There was a time when I could not let go of grudges
or resentments. I held onto them as if they were precious
gold. Even though they were causing me more harm than
the other person, I refused to forgive. My turning point
came, Lord, when you forgave me of my own character
defects. It helped me realize how the act of forgiveness
was about looking at others as a mirror for my own
behaviors. They weren't much different from me, doing
the best they could with what they knew at the time. I
can forgive them all now, and pray they forgive me, too.
Thank you, Lord, for this powerful lesson. I feel lighter,
freer, and more compassionate when I forgive others
as you forgive me.

*Therefore we are buried with him by baptism
into death: that like as Christ was raised up
from the dead by the glory of the Father,
even so we also should walk in newness of life.*

—*Romans 6:4*

*L*ord, today my heart goes out to all those whose past mistakes weigh them down and make any vision they have of their future dreary at best. Oh, that they might know you and the saving grace you bring! Draw near to them today, Lord. Reveal yourself to them in a way that will reach them, and through your mercy and forgiveness, bestow upon them a new vision—a new hope.

Then Peter said unto them, Repent,
and be baptized every one of you in the name of
Jesus Christ for the remission of sins, and ye shall
receive the gift of the Holy Ghost.

—*Acts 2:38*

Learning to forgive myself of all the mistakes I made and all the people I hurt was the hardest thing I ever did. I could forgive them, but myself? I was too busy beating myself up to see that I deserved the same compassion for myself that God had for me. I made a list of my offenses against myself, and it was a long one. Then I went to a quiet place and read each one, and forgave myself with love and empathy, as if talking to a child. It was incredibly healing and opened the door for God's Spirit to work in me in new and powerful ways.

*Better is the end of a thing than the
beginning thereof: and the patient in spirit
is better than the proud in spirit.*

—*Ecclesiastes 7:8*

*T*he people around me are irritating me, God. With an apology on my lips, help me climb out of this rut of irritation and make amends. Help me learn from my mistakes and do better. Amen.

*If we confess our sins, he is faithful and
just to forgive us our sins, and to cleanse us
from all unrighteousness.*

—*1 John 1:9*

God, I am not perfect. I continue to sin and make mistakes. Sometimes I do things that I am not proud of or that bring me nothing but a sense of shame and guilt, even though I know better at the time. I often make lousy decisions. I know it is human nature, but I aspire to be more like you in all my ways. It helps me to know that you forgive me my shortcomings, but I still pray for the wisdom, strength, and fortitude to stop having so many shortcomings to forgive. I understand life is about progress, not perfection, God. May I always do better, but when I fall short, thank you for forgiving me.

And if any man hear my words, and believe not,
I judge him not: for I came not to judge the world,
but to save the world.

—*John 12:47*

*I*f I actually sat down one day and counted how many times I judged another person for something they said or did, I would have one long list. Why is it so easy to judge others, often for things I myself say or do all the time? I guess it's easier to see my faults in someone else, reflected back to me. God, help me to stop judging, and start forgiving. Usually people don't even know they are offending me, or hurting my feelings, and I can always choose to respond differently. Inspire me, God, to have more patience and compassion with people. I think the world would be a much nicer place if we all stopped being so judgmental. Let it begin with me.

I acknowledge my sin unto thee, and mine iniquity have I not hid. I said, I will confess my transgressions unto the Lord; and thou forgavest the iniquity of my sin.

—Psalm 32:5

An honest person is not a person who never lies. There is no such person. When an honest person is caught in a lie or discovers she has lied, she is quick to admit it. She then speaks the truth. She's not afraid to say, "Please forgive me for not being honest." She does not defend a lie. Unlike a dishonest person, she does not make plans to lie or use lies to cover other falsehoods. She regularly scrutinizes her life to see if she has lied or is living a lie in any area. Honesty with God, her fellow man, and herself is the honest woman's goal and her heart's desire.

Chapter 5

Grace

• • • • • • • • • • • • • • • • • • • •

The grace of our Lord Jesus Christ be with you all. Amen.

—*Romans 16:24*

$\mathcal{W}$hen I am weak and stumble, Lord, you give me grace and sympathy instead of sermons. You show me mercy instead of meanness. You speak tenderly instead of tearing down my already-fragile ego. You are a true friend.

My grace is sufficient for thee: for my strength
is made perfect in weakness. Most gladly therefore
will I rather glory in my infirmities,
that the power of Christ may rest upon me.

—*2 Corinthians 12:9*

$\mathcal{G}$racious God, of all the gifts you give us, grace may be the most glorious! With your unmerited favor falling upon us, we can survive most anything. In times of plenty or of want, your grace is sufficient. When we feel so exhausted we don't know how we'll

get through the morning, let alone the day, your grace is sufficient. And when serious illness strikes or death is imminent, your grace is sufficient. Thank you, God, for your marvelous, glorious gift of grace.

Lord, once again I am aware that you, by your grace, gave me the strength to work through a situation that I was woefully unprepared to face. I accept that when we are completely out of ideas, drained of all energy, and so sick at heart we can barely breathe, your grace and strength lift us up and carry us forward. Thank you.

You fulfilled a promise, Lord, when you gave your Holy Spirit to live within those who dedicate their lives to you. Thank you for transforming my heart with your saving grace and for making me sensitive to your Word and your ways. You truly have brought my soul alive—as if from stone to living flesh.

And the grace of our Lord was exceeding abundant
with faith and love which is in Christ Jesus.

—1 Timothy 1:14

Heavenly Father, the joyfulness I feel inside I owe to you, for it reminds me that I'm loved and cared for, no matter how many mistakes I make today or what I do wrong. I'm your child and will forever look up to you for guidance and direction, and I will have faith that you will continue to show your everlasting love for me by providing me with just what I need when I need it. I have faith in your grace, and I hope you have faith in me to always try to do my best, knowing that even if I fall short now and then, you will love me anyway.

Grace can be a big shift, or a small adjustment, but our hearts and spirits are suddenly lifted up on wings of newfound hope, and we feel a sense of moving forward where before we were paralyzed. Fear dissipates, and faith replaces fear, while new options and ideas fill our minds with possibilities we could never have seen when we were mired in our suffering and depression. It is as if

we walked into a pitch-black room and someone suddenly turned on the lights. We can see a new way out and a new way through the challenges we thought we could not overcome.

We don't know when grace will happen, or even how it will show up in our lives, but if we have faith in God, his grace will appear just when we need it the most, reminding us that we are children of the loving Father who will never let us down and is always on our side.

*H*ow can I love God—the originator and the instigator of all love? If God is love, and he is self-sufficient, how can I possibly show him I love him? By receiving his love.

*We believe that through the grace of the
Lord Jesus Christ we shall be saved.*

—Acts 15:11

$\mathcal{L}$ord Jesus Christ, how grateful I am that—because of
your grace and not because of my own words or deeds—
you have cleansed me of my sins and offered me the
gifts of forgiveness and salvation with open arms. What

glorious, selfless gifts! Thank you for opening up the way for me to enjoy eternal life with you. I am saved only by grace through faith in you.

Thy kingdom is an everlasting kingdom, and thy dominion endureth throughout all generations. The Lord upholdeth all that fall, and raiseth up all those that be bowed down. The eyes of all wait upon thee; and thou givest them their meat in due season. Thou openest thine hand, and satisfiest the desire of every living thing. The Lord is righteous in all his ways, and holy in all his works.

—Psalm 145:13–17

*F*ather in heaven, please hear my prayer. I have faith, but I could use more. I have hope, but I could use more. I have gratitude, but I could use more. I'm not perfect, but I'm trying to be in your eyes, and I could use more help in the form of grace when I make horrible mistakes. Teach me to take things in stride, learn the lessons the first time around, and have patience and tolerance for those who test my spirit. I could use more, Lord, of all the good graces you have to give. Thank you, Father.

$\mathcal{D}$ear God, today we ask you to send your grace in abundance to all the men and women serving in our armed forces—those deployed in foreign lands and those serving in posts within our country. Through your grace, God, help them know that they are appreciated and respected. May they sense your active presence in their lives when they are put in harm's way, and may the prayers of a grateful nation fortify them. By your grace, Lord, keep them safe, and teach them to serve with honor.

Cast out the scorner, and contention shall go out; yea, strife and reproach shall cease. He that loveth pureness of heart, for the grace of his lips the king shall be his friend. The eyes of the Lord preserve knowledge, and he overthroweth the words of the transgressor.

—*Proverbs 22:10–12*

Lord, let us never miss the glimpses of grace you put in the simplest of places and deeds. A visit with an old friend in a nursing home can be bathed in your grace. A

brief exchange with someone in line can deliver a blessed amount of your grace into their day. Open our eyes to all the creative ways you are sending your grace into our world, Lord. And don't let us miss the glimpses ourselves.

He giveth grace unto the lowly.

—*Proverbs 3:34*

$\mathscr{D}$ear God, your love embraces me like the warmth of the sun, and I am filled with light. Your hope enfolds me in arms so strong, I lack for nothing. Your grace fills me with the strength I need to move through this day. For these gifts you give me—of eternal love, eternal peace, and most of all, eternal friendship—I thank you, God.

And of his fulness have all we received,
and grace for grace.

—*John 1:16*

$\mathscr{H}$eavenly Father, in our limited understanding of your generosity and of your abundant love for us, we sometimes act as if there were only a certain amount of grace to go around. We sort through our requests to determine which person is worthy of your grace or which situation should be blessed by your intervention. Forgive us for limiting you, Father. You are willing to lavish your grace upon us, and we don't want to turn away from all you want to give us. Thank you, Father, that your grace always overflows.

$\mathscr{P}$recious Lord, bless me with your grace that I may experience the deepest peace and healing only you can provide. Show me the merciful love that knows no end that I may rest today knowing I am cared for. Amen.

Then will I sprinkle clean water upon you, and ye shall be clean: from all your filthiness, and from all your idols, will I cleanse you. A new heart also will I give you, and a new spirit will I put within you: and I will take away the stony heart out of your flesh, and I will give you an heart of flesh. And I will put my spirit within you, and cause you to walk in my statutes, and ye shall keep my judgments, and do them.

—Ezekiel 36:25–27

Heavenly Father, your grace washes over me today, taking away all my impurities. I praise your name as I revel in your love. I can feel my soul shining as I turn my face to you. Please let me soak in the promise of eternal life in you, as I feel it penetrate my body to the very core. I want to carry that promise with me always, so as soon as I close my eyes, I can sense your Holy Spirit wrapped around me, holding me safe. I ask in the name of your precious son, Jesus Christ. Amen.

What is God's grace? It is the breath of God upon my face and the touch of God upon my heart, gently moving

me in the right direction. What is God's grace? It is the whisper of love in my ear and the comfort of warmth on my skin, promising that the cold, dark night is at an end. What is God's grace? It is the laughter of a child and the hugs of a friend, lifting my spirit higher. What is God's grace? It is the presence of God, who is kind, good, and loving, and to whom I can always turn.

Moreover the law entered, that the offence might abound. But where sin abounded, grace did much more abound.

—*Romans 5:20*

I know it's true, Lord. Because of your presence in my life the sins that had so much control over me in the past

119

aren't the least bit enticing anymore. You orchestrated that change in me, by your grace, and I thank you. I thank you, too, that you didn't create a long list of laws for me to follow, knowing full well I couldn't. Instead, you simply asked me to believe in you and receive the abundant provision of your grace. What a wonderful, awesome way to save me, Lord! I thank you with my whole heart.

My God, I fill my days with tasks and activities to give me status in the eyes of men and women, but I'm missing the most important fact: Because of your grace, nothing I can do can make you love me more or less. Meanwhile, help me seek your approval, not the approval of this fallen world. Let me take time from the "doing" to simply be with you, releasing myself and my life to you and your will more and more each day.

*N*one but God can satisfy the longing of the immortal soul; as the heart was made for Him, He only can fill it.

—*Richard Trench*

The Lord thy God in the midst of thee is mighty; he will save, he will rejoice over thee with joy; he will rest in his love, he will joy over thee with singing.

—*Zephaniah 3:17*

*T*oday, heavenly Father, I pray for a little more grace in my life. I could use some help from above—some small miracles today to remind me of the good in life and that I'm loved and cared for. Send down your special grace, enough for  just today, for tomorrow will take care of itself. An angel or two will do, but even if you could just spare a bit of divine guidance, I would be forever grateful. I don't need much, Father. Just a little bit of grace will do fine. Amen.

There are times in our lives when we feel alone and abandoned. Our fate seems to be a foreboding place at the end of a long, dark road. But then something happens—a simple and small miracle occurs—that brings us back to the understanding that God is always in our lives and is always ready to be of help and support when we need it. Grace is God's gift to us; it is the

blessing of his light being shined upon us as we stand in darkness. We know when God's grace has touched us because everything changes, and we change, and suddenly life seems a bit brighter and lighter than before.

And now, brethren, I commend you to God,
and to the word of his grace, which is able to build
you up, and to give you an inheritance among
all them which are sanctified.

—*Acts 20:32*

God resisteth the proud,
and giveth grace to the humble.

—*1 Peter 5:5*

$\mathcal{D}$ear Lord, it's tempting to look upon my life and feel prideful for all that I have accomplished. But everything I have has come from you, given freely to me because of your grace and not because of my actions. I go to you now in humility, reminded of my weaknesses and sins and thankful for the abundance of gifts you have given me. I am yours, pledged in your son's holy blood to obey your Word.

For all have sinned, and come short of the glory of God; Being justified freely by his grace through the redemption that is in Christ Jesus: Whom God hath set forth to be a propitiation through faith in his blood, to declare his righteousness for the remission of sins that are past, through the forbearance of God.

—Romans 3:23–25

$\mathcal{L}$ord, I know that you simply cannot be everywhere at once, so you made angels to help you spread your loving grace upon the earth. Thank you for blessing my life with an abundance of angels in the form of friends and family members who love and care for me. They fill my life with joy and give me wings to follow my dreams.

$\mathcal{O}$ God, in all I do, I want to honor you. Fill me with your grace so that I can release it into the world with each task I undertake and each person I touch. I have little to offer on my own, God, only the skills and gifts you created in me. But filled with the Holy Spirit and your grace, there's no limit to the impact my life can have. Use me, God! I want to be an ambassador of your amazing grace.

$\mathcal{C}$hrist is no Moses, no exactor, no giver of laws, but a giver of grace, a Savior; he is infinite mercy and goodness, freely and bountifully giving to us.

—*Martin Luther*

$\mathcal{H}$eavenly Father, bless us in this time of good fortune. Give us the grace to be grateful for newfound comforts, magnanimous among those who have less, and thoroughly giving with all we've been given. Amen.

And now, Lord, behold their threatenings: and grant unto thy servants, that with all boldness they may speak thy word, By stretching forth thine hand to heal; and that signs and wonders may be done by the name of thy holy child Jesus.

—Acts 4:29–30

$\mathscr{L}$ord Jesus Christ, in you and through you all things are possible. I am asking as your dedicated servant that you allow me to do great things in your name. There is too much want and strife in this world, and I am insignificant and powerless without you. I am here, with hands open and outstretched, hoping that you will enable me to spread your grace to others. It would be my greatest joy to be able to relieve the pain of others on your behalf. Please use me to do your will.

$\mathscr{H}$eavenly Father, thank you for the grace I have received at the hands of others. I have not earned their trust or forgiveness, yet they have been given to me. Such acts of love can only be at your bidding and through your Word. Thank you for letting me long for nothing. Let me learn to love others the same way you love me, wantonly and recklessly, thinking only of them and not myself.

But grow in grace, and in the knowledge of our Lord and Saviour Jesus Christ. To him be glory both now and for ever. Amen.

—*2 Peter 3:18*

*H*eavenly Father, when I look back on my life, I see material possessions I'm proud of, awards I've achieved, and accolades I've won. But then I realize that nothing I have of value has come from the work of my hands. It's only through your unearned grace that I have a life worth living. Without you and the sacrifice of your son, Jesus Christ, I'm nothing. Please humble my heart so I may be a better Christian. Amen.

Chapter 6

Gratitude

· · · · · · · · · · · · · · · · · · · ·

I will praise thee with my whole heart:
before the gods will I sing praise unto thee.

—*Psalm 138:1*

And the Lord shall guide thee continually,
and satisfy thy soul in drought,
and make fat thy bones:
and thou shalt be like a watered garden,
and like a spring of water, whose waters fail not.

—Isaiah 58:11

Lord, how precious water is to us, and how parched and desperate we are when it's in short supply. How grateful we are that you promise us access to the living water that will never run dry! Keep us mindful of that refreshing supply today, Lord. Fill us up, for we are thirsty.

*But I will sacrifice unto thee with the voice
of thanksgiving; I will pay that that I have vowed.
Salvation is of the Lord.*

—Jonah 2:9

Isn't it funny how we make promises to God in prayer when we want something? "God, do this for me and I promise I will..." I know I do, and I don't always keep those promises. But God always keeps his vows to me, and for that I am eternally grateful. Thanks be to a God that never betrays his word. Thanks be to a God that asks us for sacrifices, but knows that we will be repaid with his grace. Thanks be to a God that demands our faith and nothing more, but rewards us with his eternal presence and unceasing love. I know in my heart that when God makes me a promise, he will keep it forever.

Every man according as he purposeth in his heart,
so let him give; not grudgingly, or of necessity:
for God loveth a cheerful giver.

—2 Corinthians 9:7

The greatest blessing comes from giving. When I give from the heart, I am doing God's will and spreading the joy he has given me. I am never left with less, because God has this wonderful way of increasing my blessings the more I share them with others. Giving fills me with a sense of gratitude for the

mysterious workings of his miracles. The more I give, the more he gives me to give. How can I not stand in awe of such a powerful God that recompenses me with double the blessings I give away? God is infinite goodness. His abundance doesn't run out. I am grateful to be a channel for the flow of God's blessings.

O give thanks unto the Lord;
for he is good;
for his mercy endureth for ever.

—1 Chronicles 16:34

Gratitude may the most highly underestimated virtue. We think of love, hope, faith, and the power of prayer and forgiveness. But how often do we stop each day and give thanks for all the blessings in our lives? Are we too focused on what we lack, what we don't have, don't want, and don't need? By opening the heart and mind to focus on gratitude, we unleash a treasure of unceasing good that's just waiting to overflow into our lives. A grateful person knows that by giving thanks, they're given even more to be thankful for.

And I will bring the blind by a way that they knew
not; I will lead them in paths that they have not
known: I will make darkness light before them,
and crooked things straight. These things will I do
unto them, and not forsake them.

—Isaiah 42:16

$\mathcal{L}$ord, how grateful I am that you are willing to go before
me to prepare the way. Even when I sense that a new
opportunity is from you and has your blessing, I've
learned I still need to stop and ask you to lead before I
take the first step. Otherwise I will stumble along in the
dark tripping over stones of my own creation! Everything
goes more smoothly when you are involved, Lord.

Take heed therefore unto yourselves,
and to all the flock, over the which the Holy Ghost
hath made you overseers, to feed the church of God,
which he hath purchased with his own blood.

—Acts 20:28

$\mathcal{L}$ord, today my heart is full of gratitude for your church.
Thank you for asking us to meet together to honor you.

What power there is in voicing our thanks and petitions together! What comfort in the outstretched arms of friends! Protect us, Lord. Keep us strong—now and in the days to come.

And all these blessings shall come on thee,
and overtake thee, if thou shalt hearken
unto the voice of the Lord thy God.

—Deuteronomy 28:2

God, how often do I wake up in the morning with complaints and worries on my mind? I usually start making a to-do list in my brain the second my eyes open, and then there is no time later to stop and reflect on anything but the long list of expectations I have for myself and others. Help me, God, to stop and breathe, just long enough to be in the present moment and look at everything I already have, without concern for what I want and don't have yet. Help me, God, to start each morning with a list of blessings I am thankful for and to carry that gratitude with me throughout the day.

Honour the Lord with thy substance, and with the firstfruits of all thine increase.

—*Proverbs 3:9*

$\mathscr{D}$ear Lord, I am blessed. Life can be difficult but it is also beautiful, and I am thankful that my husband and I have work even in difficult times. Our family has enough to eat; my children have friends who are good to them; we are healthy. In fact, good health gives me the energy to parent my children, to do the work I need to do, to support others—and

indeed, God, what are we here for if not to connect with and uplift those around us?—and to pursue passions that fulfill me. Yesterday I worked in the garden. The peppers are blooming and my cat dozed in the shade nearby. My heart was so full! God, thank you. Please help me to remember gratitude, and may I always remember to honor you with everything I have.

But he giveth more grace. Wherefore he saith, God resisteth the proud, but giveth grace unto the humble.

—James 4:6

I do things I am proud of now and then, but I have to remember that any pride I have belongs to God. It humbles me when I realize that by myself I can do nothing, but with God all things become possible. My successes are his successes. My accomplishments are his accomplishments. God, I pray you keep me humble enough to know who deserves the gratitude for all my blessings and miracles. Keep me wise enough to recognize your grace working in my life and not take credit for it myself. Pride limits me, but living in your will gives me unlimited access to the promises of the kingdom of heaven. May I remain always your humble servant, God.

From the end of the earth will I cry unto thee,
when my heart is overwhelmed: lead me to the rock
that is higher than I. For thou hast been a shelter
for me, and a strong tower from the enemy.

—*Psalm 61:2–3*

$\mathcal{L}$ord, how we want to run to you in times of need—
and how blessed we are that we always find you available.
You always take us in and calm our weary spirits. You,
O Lord, are mighty and unchangeable! At times when
everything seems shaky and uncertain, you are firm
and immovable. We praise you, Lord, for your promise
to shelter us.

And out of them shall proceed thanksgiving
and the voice of them that make merry:
and I will multiply them, and they shall not be few;
I will also glorify them, and they shall not be small.

—*Jeremiah 30:19*

$\mathcal{D}$ear Lord, I thank you for the wonderful things with which you have filled my life. I have family and friends who care, clothing to wear, food to eat, and shelter over my head. You have not only provided for me, but bountifully so. I do have my challenges, but I always

stop and reflect on the ways you've blessed me, and lo and behold, I am blessed with even more to enjoy and share with others. How awesome is it to watch blessings multiply? How amazing is it to see how you magnify my good to the point of overflowing? My heart is filled with such gratitude, Lord, for your grace and glory!

Now when Daniel knew that the writing was signed,
he went into his house; and his windows being open
in his chamber toward Jerusalem, he kneeled upon
his knees three times a day, and prayed,
and gave thanks before his God, as he did aforetime.

—*Daniel 6:10*

I pray all the time when I am suffering or facing some obstacle in life. I get on my knees and ask for God's help whenever things are not going well. For me, the challenge is to remember to pray to God in thanksgiving when everything is going well. Does God only want me to come talk with him when I have a complaint or a problem? God, I promise to come to you to celebrate blessings as well as lessons. I promise to show my gratitude as easily as I show my fears. Thank you, God, for being there no matter which way I come to you.

Now unto him that is able to do exceeding
abundantly above all that we ask or think,
according to the power that worketh in us,
Unto him be glory in the church by Christ Jesus
throughout all ages, world without end.

—*Ephesians 3:20–22*

Father, sometimes I see people who seem to have found work perfectly suited to them, and I wonder if I am fulfilling my purpose. Thank you for reminding me that you are at work in me, bringing about your purposes, which are not always clear to me. You take even small gifts—as you did with the loaves and the fishes—and you make them multiply.

Whatsoever thy hand findeth to do,
do it with thy might; for there is no work,
nor device, nor knowledge, nor wisdom,
in the grave, whither thou goest.

—*Ecclesiastes 9:10*

Today I am tired, Lord. There seem to be too many things on my to-do list and too few hours in the day. And still, I know what a blessing it is to have work to do and to live a purpose-filled life. Thank you for tasks large and small that give meaning to our days, Lord. May we always do each one as if we were doing it only for you.

Wherefore comfort yourselves together,
and edify one another, even as also ye do.

—*1 Thessalonians 5:11*

Bless those who mentor, model, and cheer me on, Lord, urging me toward goals I set, applauding as I reach them, and encouraging me to try again when I don't. Remind me to be a cheerleader. I plan to say thanks to those who are mine.

Iron sharpeneth iron;
so a man sharpeneth the countenance of his friend.

—Proverbs 27:17

God has given me friends to illuminate my path and make it smooth. They guide me when I am lost and support me when I stumble. I am so grateful.

And he shall be as the light of the morning,
when the sun riseth, even a morning without clouds;
as the tender grass springing out of the earth
by clear shining after rain.

—2 Samuel 23:4

With boldness and wonder and expectation, I greet you this morning, God of sunrise and rising dew. Gratefully, I look back to all that was good yesterday and in hope, face forward, ready for today.

For the administration of this service not only
supplieth the want of the saints, but is abundant
also by many thanksgivings unto God.

—*2 Corinthians 9:12*

$\mathscr{T}$hank you, God, for the salesclerk who took an extra moment to be gracious, for the person who delivered my mail, and for the drivers who yielded to me without hesitation. I do not know their names, but they blessed me today with their hard work and positive attitudes.

I thank God, whom I serve from my forefathers
with pure conscience, that without ceasing I have
remembrance of thee in my prayers night and day.

—*2 Timothy 1:3*

$\mathscr{L}$ord, we are so thankful to you for our families and close friends. How lonely our lives would be without them, even in this splendid world of your making! What a privilege it is to come to you every day to offer prayers for them. Day after day, I bring before you those close to me who need your special attention. If I can't sleep at night, I pray for them again. Each one is so precious to me, Lord, and I know you cherish them as well. As I think of them during the day, please consider each thought to be another small prayer.

But as many as received him,
to them gave he power to become the sons of God,
even to them that believe on his name: Which were
born, not of blood, nor of the will of the flesh,
nor of the will of man, but of God.

—John 1:12–13

Spiritual birth is amazing, Father! It's a miracle no less exciting than the birth of a baby. Your Word says that it causes even the angels in heaven to rejoice. Thank you for my own spiritual birth. It's the reason I'm praying right now and enjoying this fellowship with you. It's so good to be your child. Today I'll just bask in that reality.

And be not conformed to this world:
but be ye transformed by the renewing of your mind,
that ye may prove what is that good,
and acceptable, and perfect, will of God.

—Romans 12:2

$\mathcal{L}$ife teaches us there is evil to counter good, night to counter day, and fear to counter love. It's easy for me to get caught up in the darkness, and forget there is another side to every situation. Being grateful for every experience that comes my way teaches

me that God is always present and working for my greater good. If I experience evil, my reward will be joy and justice. If I have a bad day, the next day brings new possibilities for happiness. If I am afraid, God reminds me to come back to him, and his love overcomes my fear. Every coin has two sides—heads or tails. I am grateful to God for showing me the blessings in both.

Many, O Lord my God, are thy wonderful works
which thou hast done, and thy thoughts which are
to us-ward: they cannot be reckoned up in order unto
thee: if I would declare and speak of them,
they are more than can be numbered.

—Psalm 40:5

Lord, speak to me through these pages.
Let me hear your gentle words
Come whispering through the ages
And thundering through the world.

Challenge me and change me,
comfort me and calm me.
Completely rearrange me,
Soothe me with a psalm.

Teach me how to please you,
Show me how to live.
Inspire me to praise you
For all the love you give.

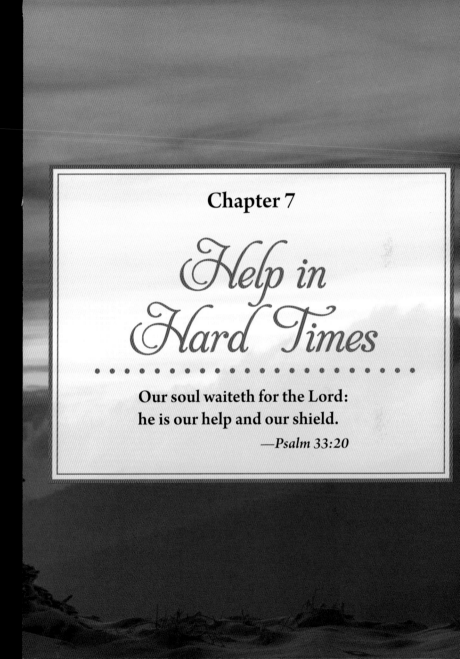

Chapter 7

Help in Hard Times

. . . .

**Our soul waiteth for the Lord:
he is our help and our shield.**

—Psalm 33:20

He staggered not at the promise of God
through unbelief; but was strong in faith,
giving glory to God.

—*Romans 4:20*

In the silence of despair, we hear nothing but the
lonely beating of our own heart. In the silence of faith,
however, rhythms of the world around us remind us that
God's heart beats nearby.

I will lift up mine eyes unto the hills,
from whence cometh my help.
My help cometh from the Lord,
which made heaven and earth.

—*Psalm 121:1–2*

Lord, you promise a helping hand in hard times. Today,
I pray for all those who are in desperate need of help in
order to survive: victims of earthquakes and tornadoes,
the homeless, and the physically and emotionally
destitute people of our world. Make yourself known to
them, Lord. May they all see that their true help comes

only from you! You who created them will not leave them without help, nor without hope.

Fear thou not; for I am with thee:
be not dismayed; for I am thy God:
I will strengthen thee; yea, I will help thee;
yea, I will uphold thee with the
right hand of my righteousness.

—Isaiah 41:10

$\mathcal{L}$ord, help me understand that the challenges I am going through serve to strengthen and empower me. Teach me the wisdom to discern that my trials mold me into something far grander than even I could have imagined.

For with God nothing shall be impossible.

—Luke 1:37

$\mathcal{I}$ am enduring a dark period, Lord. Alzheimer's disease ravages my beloved father, and I must assist him and my mother while I try to raise my own three children with strength, patience, and joy. Some nights I lie awake, filled with fear that my little family will not survive this next chapter—one of many "Sandwich Generation" families with children and parents to care for. Dear God, help me remain faithful to the promise that with you, nothing is impossible, even if I can't see through it myself.

And the work of righteousness shall be peace;
and the effect of righteousness quietness
and assurance for ever. And my people shall
dwell in a peaceable habitation, and in
sure dwellings, and in quiet resting places.

—Isaiah 32:17–18

$\mathcal{L}$ord, I want to leave the fighting behind us. It's time to restore peace to our home. Show me how to reconcile and how to be humble without being a doormat. I want the respect we have had for one another to remain intact.

The Lord is nigh unto them
that are of a broken heart; and
saveth such as be of a contrite spirit.

—Psalm 34:18

$\mathcal{W}$hen feelings are hurt, Wise Physician, we curl in on ourselves like orange rinds, withholding even the possibility of reconciliation. Help us open up to new possibilities for righting wrong and sharing love without reservation, as the orange blossom offers its fragrance, the fruit of its zesty sweetness.

*For I will restore health unto thee, and
I will heal thee of thy wounds, saith the Lord.*

—*Jeremiah 30:17*

𝓛ord, thank you for paying attention. Often I feel invisible, as if my wounds are hidden from everyone. I long for someone to understand me, to recognize my situation, to see that I need a helping hand or a kind word. But I can rest in the knowledge that you see me. You know exactly what I'm up against and precisely what I need. You listen to my cries for help and hear every syllable of my prayers. And that's why I pray to you now. Lord, please take a good look at my circumstances and step in to help me. Encourage me, enliven me, and empower me.

And Moses cried unto the Lord, saying,
"Heal her now, O God, I beseech thee."

—*Numbers 12:13*

$\mathcal{L}$ord, there are people I love who are burdened. Their hearts are burdened by sorrow, or they suffer serious physical affliction. I have loved ones who are dying of cancer, and what I want to pray is that they be healed, completely. Help me to understand the many forms "healing" can take, whether a complete restoration of health, or an acceptance, an ability, to

bear the cards life has dealt. I pray for learned doctors and medicine that effectively eases pain. I pray for strength of spirit—on the part of the sufferer, but also on my part, that I might know how best to offer comfort. Healing can take so many forms; God, may your hands heal those in need.

Now therefore fear ye not:
I will nourish you, and your little ones.
And he comforted them,
and spake kindly unto them.

—*Genesis 50:21*

*M*oney is a big issue for most people, and I am no exception. Either we don't have enough, or we worry about losing what we have. We are afraid of being left homeless and destitute. But God promises he will comfort and nourish us, with material things and things no amount of money can buy. God tells us not to be afraid. Dear God, I pray to worry less, and have more faith in your promise of prosperity. Even when my wallet looks empty, I know that blessings are happening in the unseen and will soon be made manifest. You never fail to sustain and support me, God. I pray for your care and comfort in good financial times and in bad.

Be strong and of a good courage, fear not,
nor be afraid of them: for the Lord thy God,
he it is that doth go with thee;
he will not fail thee, nor forsake thee.

—*Deuteronomy 31:6*

$\mathcal{D}$ear Lord, each night the news is full of trouble. So much pain and sorrow. It makes me ache to see it all. Some nights, it seems that's all there is; this world seems sometimes so weary and heavy laden. Then I turn to you and know that you are nearest on the darkest days. And there is comfort in knowing you and that you have not forsaken us or the people whose world is presently dark.

The Lord is my rock, and my fortress,
and my deliverer; my God, my strength,
in whom I will trust; my buckler, and the
horn of my salvation, and my high tower.

—*Psalm 18:2*

𝓛ord, there are events in my life over which I have no control. But I do have a choice either to give up or endure. If I put my trust in you, who cannot fail me, I know you will give me the endurance to get through the "tough stuff" I face in this life. Thank you, Lord, for being my help, my strength, my rock, and my fortress.

There hath no temptation taken you
but such as is common to man:
but God is faithful, who will not suffer you
to be tempted above that ye are able;
but will with the temptation also make a way
to escape, that ye may be able to bear it.

—*1 Corinthians 10:13*

𝓘 never meant to be a failure, Lord, never meant to break commitments. But I am and I did. Comfort me, for

I mourn the loss of innocence that crumbled beneath the knowledge that I couldn't stay in the marriage and be okay. Forgive my failures; heal my regrets and fortify my courage. Help me grieve and go on free from toxic, wasteful hate. And as I do, help me forgive those left behind.

And straightway the father of the child cried out, and said with tears, Lord, I believe; help thou mine unbelief.

—*Mark 9:24*

ℐ need to believe beyond the present darkness, for it threatens to stop me in my tracks. Steady me, God of infinite resources, as I collect my beliefs like candles to light and move through this dark tunnel of doubt and uncertainty. Inspire me to add new truths as they reveal themselves in my life. Along the way, help my unbelief.

Ye shall seek me, and find me,
when ye shall search for me with all your heart.

—*Jeremiah 29:13*

God, today I am mired in the challenges that life can bring. My mother is losing her battle with cancer. I try to be strong and supportive—for Mom as well as for my children—but inside I feel such fear. What will I do without her? How will I help my daughters navigate this loss? I know that you are there, but I feel depleted and alone, Lord. I do not always have the strength to seek you out. Please embolden my heart to always search after your own.

For his anger endureth but a moment;
in his favour is life: weeping may endure for a night,
but joy cometh in the morning.

—*Psalm 30:5*

Lord, only you can comfort us when we grieve. The heaviness we feel at such times can make even breathing a struggle. But you, O Lord, stay close. You fill us with your peace and your comfort. You never let us retreat completely from your light into the darkness of despair. And finally, in your time, you restore joy to our souls. We are ever thankful, O Great Comforter.

Ye shall receive power, after that the Holy Ghost is come upon you: and ye shall be witnesses unto me both in Jerusalem, and in all Judaea, and in Samaria, and unto the uttermost part of the earth.

—*Acts 1:8*

I call them my "blue days": when the demands of life deplete me. On these days it's hard to imagine that I can do all the things I need to do: work, cook, clean, weed the backyard, help my son with math and my daughter to untangle a thorny problem with a friend. I feel distracted and out of sorts. You feel far away. God, help me to remember that you fill your believers with power. Help me to tap into that power so I may stride into the world with energy, purpose, and joy. Thank you for your Spirit every day, especially on days when I am down.

For my thoughts are not your thoughts, neither are your ways my ways, saith the Lord. For as the heavens are higher than the earth, so are my ways higher than your ways, and my thoughts than your thoughts.

—Isaiah 55:8–9

Are you here, Lord? I've never felt lonelier than I do in this illness. When I despair, I repeat a child's prayer or a familiar verse and feel soothed to connect with you. The simple act of praying reminds me of your presence in both sickness and health. Please help me to hold my head high so I may always feel the light of your love on my face, even in my darkest times.

*Let us therefore come boldly unto the
throne of grace, that we may obtain mercy,
and find grace to help in time of need.*

—*Hebrews 4:16*

I don't know how to explain to someone what grace is. I only know it when it happens. I've had hard times, when financial obligations or illness threatened to derail me, yet the grace of God always managed to find its way into the problem, and, before long, miracles occurred. God has a way of being there when we most need his help, not before, not after. His timing is truly divine and his mercy unfailing—and that may be the best explanation I can come up with for grace. God, thank you for the miracles of grace you have shown me and for always being right on time when I ask for your help.

And be renewed
in the spirit of your mind.

—Ephesians 4:23

*L*ife can break your heart and your spirit. I've suffered so much heartbreak lately in my relationship, I wonder if I can ever love again. Lord, I pray for eyes that can perceive the possibilities my heart cannot imagine at this time. I come to you, Lord, for strength and comfort because right now, I cannot find it within myself. Help me, Lord, be reborn with the sun tomorrow, with a refreshed mind and a renewed spirit, and a heart willing to consider opening itself to someone special again in the future. With you, Lord, I know all things are possible. Help keep my eyes on the light and not the dark. Help me look forward to what may be, and to not look back and grieve for what was.

This day is holy unto our Lord: neither be ye sorry;
for the joy of the Lord is your strength.

—*Nehemiah 8:10*

$\mathcal{L}$ord, my heart aches for my friend, who is undergoing chemotherapy. How it saps her energy. Sometimes it seems the cure is more devastating than the disease. Stay close to her in this time of healing, Lord, for I know nothing heals like the strength that comes through you. Bring her comfort, and fill her with the knowledge that she can find hope in you. I know you will lend her the strength she needs to get through this trying time.

And Sarah said,
God hath made me to laugh,
so that all that hear will laugh with me.

—Genesis 21:6

As we face these difficult and worrisome days, help us restore our funny bones, dear God above. Laughter really can be the best medicine. Humor helps rebuild and heal, sparking hope and igniting energy with which we can combat stress, ease grief, and provide new direction. Thank you for the gift of laughter, dear God, and for giving us people to laugh with, even in hard times.

*God thundereth marvellously with his voice; great
things doeth he, which we cannot comprehend.*

—*Job 37:5*

Lord, you come to us in the storm, the fire, and even in
the stillness of a quiet moment. Sometimes your message
is strong, carried on bustling angelic wings; sometimes
our spirits are nudged, our hearts lightened by the gentle
whisper of spirit voices. However you approach us, your
message is always one of tender love and compassion.
Thank you for the certainty—and the surprise—of your
holy voice.

Let love be without dissimulation.
Abhor that which is evil; cleave to that which is good.

—*Romans 12:9*

By doing good, and doing it with love, we can overcome anything. It is such a simple way to live, but it works when we stay the course and let God do his will through us and for us. We can choose to be a part of the problem, or a part of the solution, and that choice might mean looking beyond the difficulties of life and showing gratitude for the sheer fact we are alive. Changing

perspective and putting our lives back into the hands of a loving God can make all the difference. God, I ask that my will become yours and that I do all things through the same love you've unceasingly shown me. Let me be an example of how choosing love is choosing right.

Jesus saith unto him, Rise, take up thy bed, and walk.

—*John 5:8*

$\mathcal{S}$ometimes I am afraid. Sometimes the path before me seems almost impossible. Last year, I decided to return to school. The office where I work indicated that I would have a better chance of advancing if I pursued a graduate degree. But I was anxious. School has never been easy for me, and at this stage of my life, I have myriad responsibilities, including two active children under the age of five. But I prayed about it, and worked with my husband to figure out a humane course schedule that makes sense for our family.

Though it will take a long time, I will eventually earn my degree. This first year I have been gratified to learn that I can keep up with my coursework and still make time for my job and family. It isn't always easy, though, and I pray for help every day. I have learned that if I have faith, God will help me take on enormous challenges.

Chapter 8

Hope

- -

The Lord is my portion, saith my soul;
therefore will I hope in him.

—*Lamentations 3:24*

Let us hold fast the profession of our faith without wavering; (for he is faithful that promised).

—Hebrews 10:23

Almighty God, I know you are supremely faithful! Today I ask you to restore hope to the hopeless. Plant seeds of hope in hearts that have lain fallow for so long. Send down showers of hope on those struggling with illness, persecution, or difficult relationships. Hope that comes from you is hope with the power to sustain us when nothing around us seems the least bit hopeful.

Blessed is the man that trusteth in the Lord, and whose hope the Lord is.

—Jeremiah 17:7

Living in difficult times requires us to maintain a positive, hopeful attitude about the future. Having hope is vital for our mental, physical, and spiritual health. Lord, help me move into the future with a steadfast spirit, looking forward in faith and hope and trusting in the promises you have made to your people.

Beloved, thou doest faithfully whatsoever
thou doest to the brethren, and to strangers;
We therefore ought to receive such,
that we might be fellowhelpers to the truth.

—3 John 1:5, 8

Galvanize me into prevention, intervention, and rebuilding your world, Creator God. Kids need fixers, not just worriers and those prone to panic. They need to hear plans, not just alarms. Let hope, not fear, be the last word in the bedtime stories I tell.

But, beloved, be not ignorant of this one thing,
that one day is with the Lord as a thousand years,
and a thousand years as one day.

—*2 Peter 3:8*

*W*hen trouble strikes, O God, small signs of hope
found in ordinary places restore us: friends, random
kindness, shared pain and support. Help us collect them
like mustard seeds that can grow into a spreading harvest
of well-being.

Wherefore gird up the loins of your mind, be sober,
and hope to the end for the grace that is to be brought
unto you at the revelation of Jesus Christ.

—*1 Peter 1:13*

*F*ather, your Word makes it clear to me that the life
of faith is not passive. While we wait for you to answer
prayer, grant wisdom, and open doors, we also keep our
minds sharp and our hearts strengthened by reading and
studying your Word, by meeting with you in prayer, and
by finding encouragement among other believers. These

are the disciplines our souls need to stay focused on your
ever-present hope.

Therefore if any man be in Christ,
he is a new creature: old things are passed away;
behold, all things are become new.

—*2 Corinthians 5:17*

Guide me, O God, as I encourage the children to be
positive—to see the good in each day—each person in
their classrooms, in new friends, in each challenge. Hope
and optimism are gifts from your hand that can guide
them for life.

But let us, who are of the day, be sober,
putting on the breastplate of faith and love;
and for an helmet, the hope of salvation.

—*1 Thessalonians 5:8*

can easily spend an hour just thinking about what to wear on my body, but rarely do I think about clothing myself with faith, love, and hope. Imagine what life would be like if I always put those things on first, before going out to face the challenges of my day? Those three adornments serve as my channel to the direct flow of God's love for me, and protect me from the negative energy and difficult people I come in contact with. God, let me wear my hope, faith, and love like a divinely inspired suit of armor.

The Lord also shall roar out of Zion, and utter his voice from Jerusalem; and the heavens and the earth shall shake: but the Lord will be the hope of his people, and the strength of the children of Israel.

—Joel 3:16

Today I make a covenant to you that I will choose hope. If I encounter disappointment, I will choose hope. If confronted with temptation, I will choose hope. In the face of fear, I will choose hope. If I sense doubt washing over me, I will choose hope. If I feel angry, I will choose hope. Instead of giving in to sadness or despair, I will choose hope. In all things that come my way today, Lord, I am determined to choose hope. Regardless of what happened in the past, today—through you—I am strong enough to choose hope.

Be of good courage,
and he shall strengthen your heart,
all ye that hope in the Lord.

—*Psalm 31:24*

Losing a loved one is never easy. I've always been the strong person in the family, able to handle things while everyone around me fell apart. But sometimes I lose my way and feel like I could break down. That is when I have to look deep within my heart to find courage and resilience, because death brings out all my deepest fears. That is when I must turn to God to be my hope and my comforter, and to hold me up when I feel like falling. My hope is rewarded with God's love, and allows me to become strong again and help my family cope with the loss in the most loving and caring manner possible. My hope is God.

According to my earnest expectation and my hope,
that in nothing I shall be ashamed, but that
with all boldness, as always, so now also
Christ shall be magnified in my body,
whether it be by life, or by death.

—*Philippians 1:20*

The thing I love most about having hope is the promise of that hope being realized one day. God promises me that my hopeful expectations will be fulfilled if I stay on his path, and follow his will. I have no reason to be afraid, feel guilty,

or be ashamed when I have hope, because God sees my heart and comes through...always. Thank you, God, for never giving me false hope. Thank you for never breaking your promise of reward, either in this life or the next. May my whole life be a testament of the power of hope to others, God, encouraging them to walk with joyful expectation.

But the men marvelled, saying, What manner of man
is this, that even the winds and the sea obey him!

—*Matthew 8:27*

We know you, Lord, in the changing seasons: in leaves blazing gently in fall beauty; in winter's snow sculptures. We know you in arid desert cactus blooms and in migration of whale and spawn of fish and turtle. In the blending of the seasons, we feel your renewing, steadfast care, and worries lose their power to overwhelm. The list of your hope-filled marvels is endless, and our gratitude equally so.

In all these things we are more than conquerors
through him that loved us.

—*Romans 8:37*

$\mathcal{L}$ord, I'm looking forward to this new phase of my life. It is full of promise and hope, though I know that challenges will surely come as well. I know you have all the courage, strength, faithfulness, and love I need to meet each moment from a perspective of peace. I just need to stay tethered to you in prayer, listening for your Spirit to guide me and turn my thoughts continually back toward you. That's the key to a good life.

I wait for the Lord, my soul doth wait,
and in his word do I hope.

—Psalm 130:5

$\mathcal{H}$elp me to slow down, God of patience, because sometimes I'm so frustrated by this tough daily grind. I know you have a plan for me and I see your good works in my life and those of my loved ones. But it's hard to keep my mind clear of negative clutter when I'm in my routine, caring for my spouse or children, going to work, feeling stuck. In your Word I find moments of peace, the promise of quietude.

For we are saved by hope:
but hope that is seen is not hope:
for what a man seeth, why doth he yet hope for?

—*Romans 8:24*

It's easy to believe in something I can see and feel, something tangible I have proof of. God asks me to have hope for things I cannot see, and to hold fast to hope no matter how long it takes to manifest into reality. I struggle with this kind of deep faith, but when I surrender to

God's will it becomes easy to imagine what is not yet real. When I live by my will, I become fixated on proof of the outcome and I want what I want and I want it now. But living in God's will allows me to hope for the possible, not just the provable, and know it will come to pass. God never fails me when I put my hope in him.

*They that wait upon the Lord shall renew
their strength; they shall mount up with wings
as eagles; they shall run, and not be weary;
and they shall walk, and not faint.*

—Isaiah 40:31

$\mathcal{L}$ord, let me be strong today, drawing my courage from my hope in you. Help me lean not on my own strength but on your limitless power. I know there is work to be done—burdens to be lifted, temptations to be resisted, and unkindness to be forgiven. Let my thoughts and actions be motivated by the hope generated by your promises.

For thou art my hope, O Lord God:
thou art my trust from my youth.

—*Psalm 71:5*

$\mathcal{L}$ittle children automatically see the good and look for the silver linings. Kids have such hope built into their personalities. I recall when I was young, I had faith and hope that all would be well, even when my parents or family suffered some illness, job loss, or other hardship. I just had that seed of hope in my heart. Now that I am older, I find my hope in God and his presence and love. I still feel that sense of goodness and that all will be well when I am centered in hope and in him. If I keep my heart open, as I did when I was little, and come to God for help, he never fails to give me what I need.

Therefore being justified by faith,
we have peace with God
through our Lord Jesus Christ:
By whom also we have access by faith
into this grace wherein we stand,
and rejoice in hope of the glory of God.

—*Romans 5:1–2*

$\mathcal{S}$pirit, help me live one day at a time so that I may meet each day's challenges with grace, courage, and hope. Shelter me from the fears of the future and the anguish of the past. Keep my mind and heart focused on the present, where the true gift of happiness and healing is to be found.

Hope deferred maketh the heart sick:
but when the desire cometh, it is a tree of life.

—*Proverbs 13:12*

$\mathcal{W}$e all know the sting of being heartsick. Loss, unrequited love, unfulfilled expectations —any of these can lead to the feeling of our heart being sick. This passage above tells us that it is actually deferring, or putting off, hope that truly makes our hearts sick. God knows the pain we experience in this life. He knows how to comfort us. If we cling to hope and turn to God, despite all that life may throw at us, we are sure to find ourselves filled with peace and joy.

The hope of the righteous shall be gladness:
but the expectation of the wicked shall perish.

—*Proverbs 10:28*

$\mathcal{I}$ see people every day doing wrong and bringing harm to others, and benefiting from it. I see good people suffering and losing everything, and I wonder where the justice is. Lord, help me remember your justice happens on a much higher level and that the hope of the good is always rewarded, while the motives of the evil are always

 judged and accounted for. Let me not have any expectations that come from a place of selfishness or greed, but help me, Lord, to always hope to be my best, and do my best, for myself and others. If I walk the right path, I may still suffer, but I know my ultimate reward will be joy. May I always walk the right path, Lord.

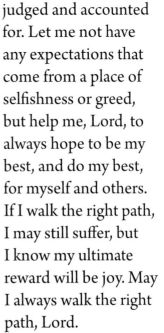

And our hope of you is stedfast, knowing,
that as ye are partakers of the sufferings,
so shall ye be also of the consolation.

—2 Corinthians 1:7

Why me, Lord? I have asked that question a million times, when I become ill, or one of my children is hurt. Why me, Lord? And his answer? Why not you? I learned the Lord doesn't pick and choose who suffers. We all suffer at some point in life, and no one is immune. But I also learned whatever suffering the Lord asks

me to experience comes with the courage, strength, and compassion to get through it. It's a promise the Lord made to me, that he would never give me more than I could handle. So when things come into my life I'd rather not deal with, I have hope and faith that I can deal with them, with the Lord to guide me.

And thou shalt be secure, because there is hope;
yea, thou shalt dig about thee, and thou
shalt take thy rest in safety.

—*Job 11:18*

Without hope, life would be dark and meaningless. Hope reminds me of a lighthouse beacon that leads ships safely back to shore, especially during storms. I recall so many times, God, when having hope got me through my feelings of anxiety and depression. Having hope in you, God, was the lifeline that kept my head above water and gave me a sense of comfort even on the most stormy, uncomfortable days. Thank you, God, for proving to me that my sense of hope in you was never misplaced, and always led to the courage and strength necessary to overcome life's emotional dramas and painful challenges. Thank you, God, for helping me to keep hope alive in my heart.

The Lord is my light and my salvation;
whom shall I fear? the Lord is the strength
of my life; of whom shall I be afraid?

—Psalm 27:1

In the midst of the darkness that threatens to overwhelm us lies a pinpoint of light, a persistent flicker that guides us through the pain and fear, through the hopelessness and despair, to a place of peace and healing on the other side. This is God's Spirit, leading us back home like the lighthouse beacon that directs the ships through the fog to the safety of the harbor.

Chapter 9

Comfort

Comfort thine heart, I pray thee.

—*Judges 19:8*

*Let, I pray thee, thy merciful kindness be for my
comfort, according to thy word unto thy servant.*

—*Psalm 119:76*

$\mathcal{L}$ord, today I ask you to comfort the elderly among us.
No matter how old we are, we notice our bodies aging.
How difficult it must be to be near the end of life and
struggling to hold on to mobility, vision, hearing, and
wellness of being. Give us compassion for those older
than we are, Lord, and thank you for your promise that
you will be with us to the very end of our days.

*For thou hast been a strength to the poor, a strength
to the needy in his distress, a refuge from the storm,
a shadow from the heat, when the blast of the terrible
ones is as a storm against the wall.*

—*Isaiah 25:4*

$\mathcal{W}$hen the storms of life rage around me, Lord, I know
that I can seek refuge in your loving grace. You are a
beacon guiding me through the thick fog of fear and
confusion to the safe comfort of the shore. Steady and

true are your love and your strength. Steadfast and secure am I in the light of your changeless and timeless presence that permeates the darkest of nights.

Thou shalt increase my greatness,
and comfort me on every side.

—*Psalm 71:21*

There is a comfort only God can provide, a food for the soul and drink for the heart that quenches all sense of emptiness and loneliness. All too often, we seek comfort in things outside of ourselves, in the confines and limitations of the material world. But there already exists a comfort that needs no seeking; it needs only recognition. God's love fills us, but we have to acknowledge its presence within. God's comfort embraces us on every side, but we have to first quiet our anxious minds and silence our inner chatter to feel God's comfort wrapped around us. There is no need to look outside ourselves for comfort. God's comfort has been within us all along.

I will not leave you comfortless: I will come to you.

—*John 14:18*

*T*hank you, Holy God, for your comfort in my time of need. Even when I am empty and near hopelessness, I know that you are there, eternal and gracious, giving me the will and strength to try again. Your love is a solace and a refuge, and I return to you over and over, seeking the renewing power of your Holy Spirit. Your grace refreshes and restores me, and I kneel at your feet in thanksgiving. Amen.

Blessed are they that mourn:
for they shall be comforted.

—*Matthew 5:4*

O Lord of all, only you know how deeply I am grieving. There are days when I don't know if I can get my breath, let alone face my responsibilities with a clear mind and a willing spirit. Come into my pain and mourning, Lord. Begin your miraculous healing from the inside out, because without you, I honestly don't think I'll survive this. Send your comfort, Lord, and caress me with your compassion.

 Lord Almighty, what comfort I find in your constancy and faithfulness. You are the same God who hung the stars in the universe and called them by name. You've heard the prayers of troubled souls since the beginning of time, and yet you never stop listening. Thank you, Lord, for your constant sovereignty and your unfailing love. You are our comfort and our strength when everything around us seems to be falling apart.

My soul, wait thou only upon God; for my expectation is from him. He only is my rock and my salvation: he is my defence; I shall not be moved. In God is my salvation and my glory: the rock of my strength, and my refuge, is in God.

—*Psalm 62:5–7*

God, when all else fails I know that I can count on you to be my fortress and my foundation. I give thanks each day for the steadfast comfort you provide, and I pray that you will give this same comfort to those who suffer in fear and silence today. Give to them the same freedom from worry as you did me, by showing them the same mercy and love you show me each day. Be their fortress just as you are mine so that they, too, may understand they never walk alone. Amen.

God, I am hurting today. All the wounds I've received in this lifetime seem open and raw, and only the balm of your love can comfort me. I need you to take me in your hands, fill me with your Holy Spirit, and ease all the aching, lonely places as only you can. I know that your power is endless and your love is

merciful, and I have faith in your all-healing presence. I pray that all my worries and cares will be washed away from me, just like my sins were taken from me by the death of your son, Jesus Christ. Amen.

$\mathcal{F}$or it is only the finite that has wrought and suffered; the infinite lies stretched in smiling repose.

—*Ralph Waldo Emerson*

$\mathcal{L}$ord Jesus, it is so easy to seek comfort from material things—from a new car or sofa, from a trip to the mall or from the movies. But you are not found in worldly things. The only true source of everlasting comfort is your love, the living water you offer us from your very lips. Let me remember to seek first your will, perfect and divine. It is only then that my weary heart will rest and find sanctuary. Amen.

$\mathcal{G}$od, let me be a comfort to someone who needs me today. As you have always comforted me in rough times, let me do the same for someone who is sad, ill, or suffering and needs to know they are cared for. Guide me toward those I can be of loving service to, and let no opportunity pass me to do something good in the world today. If someone is in need, send him my way. If someone is depressed, have her call me. Let me be a comfort to those who feel they cannot go on alone. I am at your service today, God. Make use of me. Amen.

$\mathcal{G}$od, I surrender to you this will of mine and offer to you my faith and trust. For far too long I have tried to control my life, and it has never worked out well. Instead, I was left feeling adrift on an ocean of anxiety and worry, looking for dry land and not seeing it. Then you remind-ed me that dry land is right where I am, right where you are, and that I am never alone. If I just let go and let you take the controls, my life will hum along smoothly. All I need to do is enjoy the ride in comfort. No longer shall I fight to maintain control, but I will give over my life to the one who knows best. Amen.

$\mathcal{L}$ove comforteth like sunshine after rain.

—*William Shakespeare*

$\mathcal{D}$ear heavenly Father, when I was a child, I went to my mother for comfort. She held me in her lap, rocked me close to her heart, and wiped my tears away. As I grew older, suddenly I was the parent and had no one to turn to for shelter. That is when I learned that you are my loving father, my Abba, who will always hold me close, just as my mother once did. No matter how old I grow, I can still feel the safety of a child held in loving arms, comforted and loved beyond all measure. I know that I am yours, a child of God, who you know by name and love for all eternity. Amen.

He healeth the broken in heart, and bindeth up their wounds. Great is our Lord, and of great power: his understanding is infinite. The Lord lifteth up the meek: he casteth the wicked down to the ground.

—*Psalm 147:3, 5–6*

$\mathcal{L}$ord, I pray that my words and actions may be a comfort to those in need. Let me see the world around me through your eyes, that I might notice the small wounds and sorrows that each of us carries within us, hidden from view and known only to you. I ask that you use my hands to do your work here on Earth, to heal the hurting, to feed the hungry, to befriend the lonely. May I be an instrument of your endless love, that I might share your Spirit generously and abundantly with everyone I encounter.

Jesus Christ the same yesterday,
and to day, and for ever.

—Hebrews 13:8

ℒord Jesus Christ, what comfort we find in your changeless nature. When we look back and remember all the ways you've guided us in the past, we know we have no need to be anxious about the future. You were, are, and will always be our Savior and Lord. Why should we fear instability when you are always here with us?

Chapter 10

Joy

● ●

And my soul shall be joyful in the Lord: it shall rejoice in his salvation.

—Psalm 35:9

The statutes of the Lord are right,
rejoicing the heart: the commandment of the
Lord is pure, enlightening the eyes.

—*Psalm 19:8*

$\mathcal{L}$ord, so much joy exists in your truth. Those who
say your commands and guidelines are restrictive or
oppressive simply haven't taken them to heart. Once we
accept that your guidance is always in our best interest,
we discover the amazing freedom that exists within a
life of faith. Thank you for speaking to us through your
Word, Lord. We are entirely grateful for the peace, contentment, and the heartfelt joy that your Word gives us.

$\mathcal{I}$s joy as elusive as a butterfly? It's easy for many of us
to get excited, feel passionate, and be happy. But is it just
as easy to experience joy? In fact, what causes us to feel
joy? The Bible answers that question: People feel joy
when they are in God's hands, sensing the force of God's
love, grace, compassion, and mercy at work in their lives.

$\mathcal{P}$erhaps we feel joy more often than we think. When our children are born and we look into their eyes for the very first time, is that not joy? When we gaze out at a glorious sunset over the vast expanse of the ocean, or when we look up at the desert night sky and stand in awe of our tiny place in a universe so big we cannot comprehend it, are those not moments of joy? Maybe

it's when we first fall in love, or first achieve a major life goal, or come back from a horrible disease or trauma. When God blesses us in those ways, surely we feel exceedingly joyful.

Joy is the opening up of the heart—the expansion of the soul. It is fleeting, but that's what makes it so precious and profound. If we were to feel joy all the time, we would not appreciate it when we do feel it. Joy cracks us open at our very core and exposes us to the connectedness of all things, but even more importantly, to our intimate relationship with God.

$\mathcal{J}$oy is magic, awe, wonder, and the lifting of our spirit into God's forgiveness and redemption. And when our spirit is lifted from our burdens and sins, that's when we take flight. It is then that God brings us his special, heavenly joy and that our being soars with that elusive butterfly.

Be glad in the Lord, and rejoice, ye righteous:
and shout for joy, all ye that are upright in heart.

—*Psalm 32:11*

$\mathcal{L}$ord, you are the source of all joy! Regardless of how happy we may feel at any given time, we know happiness is fleeting. Happiness, so dependent on temporary circumstances, is fickle and unpredictable. But joy in you is forever! And so we come to you today, Lord, rejoicing in all you were, all you are, and all you will ever be. Because of you, we rejoice!

*T*hankful hearts are joyful hearts, and joyful hearts seek to give praise to God. But what qualifies as praise? Do you need a good singing voice? Are there certain "approved" statements? What is the protocol? While singing is certainly one aspect of praise, thankfully for some of us, golden vocals are not required. In the Bible's own words, "a joyful noise" is a perfectly acceptable tribute to God for the good things he's done. "Let us come before his presence with thanksgiving, and make a joyful noise unto him with psalms" (Psalm 95:2).

And these things write we unto you,
that your joy may be full.

—1 John 1:4

*M*y mother was a joyful person. She faced challenges like everyone else—her health in particular troubled her

off and on through most of her adult life—but as a rule, she chose to focus on the positive. Her joyful outlook took many forms—she was a calm, good listener; she embraced new experiences; she was interested and interesting. And something that strikes me now is how her radiant spirit was often contagious. I myself would sometimes return from school glum or discouraged, but if we spent some quiet time together—working in the garden, say, or sometimes I would finish my homework in the kitchen while Mom cooked dinner—my own spirits lifted. Mom died last year, and as an adult, I am left to carry her bright torch for my own family. God, help me to always remember how important it is to share our joy with others so that they may experience it.

There can be no experience of joy without first having faith in God. Our faith acts as a trigger that frees us from the anxieties, worries, and concerns that bog down our happiness and keep our bliss blocked at its source. God is always ready to bless us, but it's first up to us to do our part to clear the way for those blessings to arrive. Then we get to know how it feels to live with joy.

*W*ith an eye made quiet by the power of harmony and the deep power of joy, we see into the lives of things.

—*William Wordsworth*

Deceit is in the heart of them that imagine evil:
but to the counsellors of peace is joy.

—*Proverbs 12:20*

That I may come unto you with joy by the will of
God, and may with you be refreshed.

—Romans 15:32

*T*oday, Lord, I make a request, not for myself, but for someone else I care about. You know the struggles this dear one has gone through, along with the usual doubts and questions. What I ask for this loved one is joy.

Provide a deep sense of satisfaction in your presence, dear Lord. Whisper your wooing and shout your power. Fill this person's world with wonder. Resurrect the dead parts of this person's soul and offer a new kind of life, overflowing with laughter. Bring joy to this joyless heart.

*Y*our joy surprises me, Lord. Just when I think I have you figured out, something happens that shatters my assumptions. It's then that your joy taps me on the shoulder and takes me on a new journey. Thank you, Lord!

$\mathcal{R}$emember, in the first place, that the Vine was the Eastern symbol of Joy. It was its fruit that made glad the heart of man. Yet, however innocent that gladness—for the expressed juice of the grape was the common drink at every peasant's board—the gladness was only a gross and passing thing. This was not true happiness, and the vine of the Palestine vineyards was not the true vine. "Christ was the true Vine." Here, then, is the ultimate source of Joy. Through whatever media it reaches us, all true Joy and Gladness find their source in Christ.

—*Henry Drummond*

Strengthened with all might, according to
his glorious power, unto all patience
and longsuffering with joyfulness.

—*Colossians 1:11*

$\mathcal{H}$eavenly Father, we confess that it's not easy for us to embrace the hard times. When finances are tight, relationships are strained, or children are ill, it can be extremely difficult to feel joyful. Yet we know that the joy that comes from our relationship with you can outshine any darkness. Keep us joyful, Lord, whatever our circumstances. Don't let us become so mired down by the discouraging aspects of life that we lose sight of the abiding, eternal joy that is ours in you.

*W*hen we think of joy, we often think of things that are new—a new day, a new baby, a new love, a new beginning, the promise of a new home with God in heaven. Rejoicing in these things originates with having joy in God who makes all things new. Rather than relying on earthly pleasures to provide happiness, the scriptures command us to rejoice in God and in each new day he brings. Joy is a celebration of the heart that goes beyond circumstances to the foundation of joy— the knowledge that God loves us.

A woman when she is in travail hath sorrow,
because her hour is come: but as soon as she is
delivered of the child, she remembereth no more the
anguish, for joy that a man is born into the world.

—*John 16:21*

$\mathcal{J}$oy eludes us, just out of reach, until we shift our focus from what we feel is lacking in our lives to the wonderful blessings we have been given. Just a small change in perspective can open our eyes and our hearts to the feeling of joyfulness. Suddenly, we forget our sorrows.

$\mathcal{J}$oy is not gush; joy is not jolliness. Joy is perfect acquiescence in God's will because the soul delights in God himself.

—*H. W. Webb-Peploe*

$\mathcal{J}$oy will always return to those who love God. We may find ourselves brought low by some of life's difficulties—and certainly by the tragedies that take us by storm. But none of these—not even the tragedies—can rob us of the deep-seated joy we have in our God. "Weeping may endure for a night, but joy cometh in the morning" (Psalm 30:5). We may weep, even as Jesus did at times, but like him, we have a future joy set before us that no struggle on this earth can undermine or destroy. Our morning lies just ahead.

And the angel said unto them, Fear not: for, behold, I bring you good tidings of great joy, which shall be to all people.

—Luke 2:10

Joy grows in the most unlikely of places. It reaches up in the middle of poverty to dance in the eye of a child at play. It spreads itself across the face of an old man whose illness is forgotten the moment he greets an old friend. Joy wedges itself through the cracks of loneliness when the voice at the other end of the phone line is that of someone familiar and loved. Joy is found where it is least expected, because true joy roots itself not in the shifting sands of circumstance but in the rich soil of a grateful heart.

*H*appiness seems made to be shared.

—*Jean Racine*

Make a joyful noise unto the Lord, all the earth:
make a loud noise, and rejoice, and sing praise.

—*Psalm 98:4*

I celebrate you, dear Lord, and all that you have given me. I'm filled with a sense of pure joy as I look around at the wonderful people and things you have brought into my life. From my friends and family to the place I call home, I've been truly blessed with wonderful things, and I owe all of those good things to you. Thank you for showing me heaven on Earth and for bringing joy into my life each and every day. Amen.

The joy of God be in thy face,
Joy to all who see thee,
The circle of God around thy neck,
Angels of God shielding thee,
Angels of God shielding thee.
Joy of night and day be thine,
Joy of sun and moon be thine,
Joy of men and women be thine.
Each land and sea thou goest,
Each land and sea thou goest.
Be every season happy for thee,
Be every season bright for thee,
Be everyone glad for thee.
Thou beloved one of my breast,
Thou beloved one of my heart.

—*Celtic Prayer*

I will greatly rejoice in the Lord, my soul shall be joyful in my God; for he hath clothed me with the garments of salvation, he hath covered me with the robe of righteousness, as a bridegroom decketh himself with ornaments, and as a bride adorneth herself with her jewels.

—Isaiah 61:10

We trust the Lord when we are sad, and in due season He so answers our confidence that our faith turns to fruition and we rejoice in the Lord. Doubt breeds distress, but trust means joy.

—Charles Spurgeon

Let all those that seek thee rejoice and be glad in thee:
and let such as love thy salvation say continually,
Let God be magnified. But I am poor and needy:
make haste unto me, O God: thou art my help and
my deliverer; O Lord, make no tarrying.

—Psalm 70:4–5

O Lord, how I love to praise you with all my heart! Joyful music pervades my day, whether at home or in the car. The deeply significant passages of the old hymns and the contemporary lyrics of modern praise songs all have the ability to refocus me and bring me to tears of joy. May the gift of praise always draw me closer to you, Lord, until I join that choir of millions praising you in your heavenly kingdom.

The heart first feels the gentle nudge of hope. Light shines in the cracked and broken places, turning the nudge into a dance of faith and trust. Then the heart bursts open and feels an incredible sense of release of all worries and concerns. This is joy. But it all begins first with hope.

$\mathcal{W}$e find delight in the beauty and happiness of children that makes the heart too big for the body.

—*Ralph Waldo Emerson*

$\mathcal{G}$od, you instruct us to come to you for everything we seek, and yet, I feel this sense of discontent that I don't understand and cannot seem to shake. I want nothing more than to fully know the joy that comes from surrendering to your will. I want nothing more than to achieve that sense of inner peace that only comes from being touched by your merciful love and grace. Let me know this joy and this peace today, dear God.

The meek also shall increase their joy in the Lord,
and the poor among men shall rejoice in the
Holy One of Israel.

—*Isaiah 29:19*

God, now I understand why you ask great things of me, and why you often give me more than I think I can handle. It's so that when I do overcome those obstacles and meet those challenges, I can feel the joy of achievement and accomplishment. I can feel the joy of knowing that with your everlasting love and presence, there's no mountain I cannot move and no stormy sea I cannot calm. The problems of life are my opportunities to find joy and to know that I can do anything with you, God.

The root of faith produces the flower of heart-joy. We may not at the first rejoice, but it comes in due time. We trust the Lord when we are sad, and in due season He so answers our confidence that our faith turns to fruition and we rejoice in the Lord. Doubt breeds distress, but trust means joy in the long run...

Let us meditate upon the Lord's holy name, that we may trust Him the better and rejoice the more readily. He is in character holy, just, true, gracious, faithful and unchanging. Is not such a God to be trusted? He is allwise, almighty, and everywhere present; can we not cheerfully rely on Him?...They that know thy name will trust thee; and they that trust thee will rejoice in thee, O Lord.

—*Charles Spurgeon*

Thou hast turned for me my mourning into dancing: thou hast put off my sackcloth, and girded me with gladness; To the end that my glory may sing praise to thee, and not be silent. O Lord my God, I will give thanks unto thee for ever.

—*Psalm 30:11–12*

$\mathscr{O}$ Lord, after a long period of grief, how surprised we are by joy! It begins with a smile, an unexpected hug from a friend, or a precious memory. Soon we dare to

221

believe that we really will survive the darkest period of grief because the true joy that sustains us—your joy—will return to save us. Thank you, Lord, that we don't have to suffer the raw agony of grief longer than we can bear it. Thank you for sending your joy.

God's strength is a source of joy. The 1981 movie *Chariots of Fire* portrayed Scotland's Eric Liddell's gold-medal race in the 1924 Olympics. Believing his swiftness and strength were from God, Liddell said that when he ran, he felt God's pleasure. The humble athlete's races were, for him, an act of exuberant praise to God for the strength he had given him. "Be thou exalted, Lord, in thine own strength: so will we sing and praise thy power" (Psalm 21:13). God manifests his strength in many ways, within us and beyond us, each display a source of joy and opportunity for praise.

I have no greater joy than to hear that
my children walk in truth.

—*3 John 1:4*

$\mathscr{L}$ord, how joyful I feel today, for the past is behind me and I'm facing a bright and beautiful future. Thanks to your presence and constant compassion, I have overcome great challenges, and now I feel strong and fully alive as I take on a whole new life. You, dear Lord, have recreated me, and now I truly feel as though my life has meaning and purpose. I'm here for a reason, and I now ask that you reveal that reason to me and let me go out and spread this joy to others. Amen.

Make a joyful noise unto the God of Jacob.

—*Psalm 81:1*

$\mathcal{E}$very saint in heaven is as a flower in the garden of God, and every soul there is as a note in some concert of delightful music.

—*Jonathan Edwards*

And Jesus answering saith unto them, Have faith in God. For verily I say unto you, That whosoever shall say unto this mountain, Be thou removed, and be thou cast into the sea; and shall not doubt in his heart, but shall believe that those things which he saith shall come to pass; he shall have whatsoever he saith.

—*Mark 11:22–23*

My God, my joy is my faith, and I'm filled each day with gratitude and awe at the power of your presence and the wonder of your miracles. You have never abandoned me, even when I was in my darkest hours. You have never walked away from me, no matter what sin I've committed. I'm bursting with joy at the realization that you're my loving, caring, forgiving Father, who is always looking out for me. Amen.

Blessed is the people that know the joyful sound: they shall walk, O Lord, in the light of thy countenance.

—*Psalm 89:15*

Heavenly Father, what can be more joyful than to realize that through you, all things are possible? Even when I'm at the lowest point in my life, I only have to reach out to you, and you take me and lift me up again. Though there is much trouble and hardship in my life right now, my joy is knowing that you have reserved a place for me in your heavenly kingdom. Thank you, Father.

When I think of God, my heart is so full of joy that the notes leap and dance as they leave my pen: and since God has given me a cheerful heart, I serve him with a cheerful spirit.

—*Franz Joseph Haydn*

Let the field be joyful, and all that is therein:
then shall all the trees of the wood rejoice
Before the Lord: for he cometh, for he cometh to
judge the earth: he shall judge the world with
righteousness, and the people with his truth.

—*Psalm 96:12–13*

Lord, on days when I'm privileged to be out walking in the beautiful world you created, I sometimes feel as if all the plants and animals are celebrating their creation with you. If only we humans were as joyful, it would be simply marvelous! Thank you, Lord, for the glory of your creation and the reminder it brings that this is truly your world, and you will return to redeem it.

O let the nations be glad and sing for joy:
for thou shalt judge the people righteously,
and govern the nations upon earth.

—Psalm 67:4

*H*eavenly Father, when I stop for a moment and just think about all the blessings you've showered on me, I'm filled with joy and happiness. I often complain about my problems and focus on the things I wish I had, but in these quiet moments I truly become aware of just how few problems I do have and how much you've given me. Thank you for slowing down my often hectic and crazy life every now and then so I can recognize these moments of pure joy.

*O come, let us sing unto the Lord: let us
make a joyful noise to the rock of our salvation.*

—*Psalm 95:1*

God, let me sing your praises, and let me dance with joy, for you have blessed me with so much, and I'm overflowing with gratitude today. When I needed you, you came to me and helped me solve whatever problems were set before me. When I felt lost, you showed me the path and helped me find my way back home. When I was tired and cold, you refreshed my spirit and warmed my heart. Let me sing your praises, God, for you have been my rock and my foundation. Thank you, thank you, thank you!

*And he brought forth his people with joy,
and his chosen with gladness.*

—*Psalm 105:43*

$\mathcal{L}$ord, why do other believers have such expressive joy when I don't? Is there something wrong with me? I keep hearing that we should have abundant lives, praising you all the time, but that doesn't ring true for me. Can I still love you without jumping for joy all the time? Still, I'd love to feel lighter in my faith—more simple smiles and fewer thoughtful scowls. Can I just enjoy your presence? That's what I want. Draw near to me, Lord, and teach me to smile.

$\mathcal{J}$oy is the echo of God's life within us.

—*Joseph Marmion*

But the fruit of the Spirit is love, joy, peace, longsuffering, gentleness, goodness, faith.

—*Galatians 5:22*

229

$\mathcal{L}$ord, I often thank you for things that make me happy. If I'm enjoying the weather, I thank you. If I appreciate a good friendship, I thank you. A parking place, a cappuccino, a tax refund— these are blessings I rejoice in. But I don't want to overlook what's most important—that I find fullness of joy in your presence. So thank you, my wonderful Lord, for being you. And thank you for being with me.

$\mathcal{L}$et us be grateful to people who make us happy, they are the charming gardeners who make our souls blossom.

—*Marcel Proust*

$\mathcal{L}$ord, in case we haven't remembered to thank you lately for the gifts of friendship and kinship, we thank you now. Even the worst of days is made better when we come together with those loved ones you have placed into our lives. Friendships and kinships are the blessings that allow us to share and multiply the joy in our hearts. Thank you, Lord, for placing them in our lives.

*M*irth is the sweet wine of human life. It should be offered, sparkling with zestful life, unto God.

—*Henry Ward Beecher*

And they departed quickly from the sepulchre with fear and great joy; and did run to bring his disciples word.

—*Matthew 28:8*

*L*ord Jesus, how amazing it is to me that you rose from the tomb! Even in situations that fill us with fear, we can be filled with joy. The fear comes from the unknown, but the joy comes from knowing that you've conquered death and that you will never leave us. Thank you, Lord, for the promise that nothing that happens to us will ever rob us of the real joy we have in you.

$\mathcal{L}$ord, how grateful we are for the discernment to know the difference between happiness and joy. Happiness is dependent on what happens, but joy is based on your unchangeable nature and our intimacy with you. Happiness is momentary, but joy is eternal! Help me shine the light of this truth into the lives of all those I encounter each day, Lord. For your joy is not only life-changing, but it's also contagious.

Let them shout for joy, and be glad, that favour my
righteous cause: yea, let them say continually,
Let the Lord be magnified, which hath pleasure
in the prosperity of his servant.

—*Psalm 35:27*

Fulfil ye my joy, that ye be likeminded, having the same love, being of one accord, of one mind.

—*Philippians 2:2*

Make me to hear joy and gladness; that the bones which thou hast broken may rejoice.

—*Psalm 51:8*

$\mathcal{L}$ord of life, I long for joy. Fill my soul with gladness. Let me greet each day with a song. I'm not asking you to make me blind to the serious matters of life, but keep reminding me of your presence, your guidance, and your ultimate victory. Show me the love that undergirds your creation. And awake in my heart the laughter of the universe, as I join with all nature in expressing our utter delight in you.

233

Restore unto me the joy of thy salvation;
and uphold me with thy free spirit.

—*Psalm 51:12*

𝒟ear Lord, I have known times of suffering and pain, and times of happiness and contentment, but I would like to open my heart and my spirit to know the joy only you give. I hear it spoken of all the time, and yet I don't know what it really feels like to be lost in the awe and wonder that your joy is supposed to bring. I ask in prayer that you help me do whatever I need to do to find my way to this joy. I will follow your guidance and do your will, so that I, too, can know the meaning of a joy-filled spirit. Thank you, Lord.

𝒩othing can compare, dear Lord, with the joy of waking up another day, knowing that life is full of opportunities to enjoy life and spread this joy to others. When I go to sleep each night, I'm grateful for the day I left behind. And when I awaken, I'm filled with a sense of complete renewal and faith, for you have given me the miraculous gift of a fresh new day and a fresh new chance to live it to the fullest. I'm forever grateful, Lord, for the simple gift of being alive another day. Amen.

For ye are our glory and joy.

—1 Thessalonians 2:20

 *A*lmighty God, I keep find-
ing rich nuggets of truth in
your Word. Here I find that
my strength comes not always
from holiness or earnestness
but from your glory and joy.
I've often considered joy a
frivolous thing—a good feeling easily swept away by the
more important issues of life,
but here I discover otherwise. When I find my pleasure
in you, dear God, that brings meaning to my whole life.
When I exult in your presence each day, I find energy for
every task. Strengthen me today, God, with your joy!

Yet I will rejoice in the Lord,
I will joy in the God of my salvation.

—Habakkuk 3:18

Not for that we have dominion over your faith,
but are helpers of your joy: for by faith ye stand.

—*2 Corinthians 1:24*

 oday, Lord, I lift up
to you all those who feel
that their dreams and
goals will never be real-
ized. Even those who pray
for your direction and
guidance before moving
forward can experience
unexpected setbacks and periods of discouragement
and confusion. Encourage them, Lord. Remind them
that they can endure in the midst of failure and find the
gumption to try one more time. Give them your strength
and joy, Lord, for we know that in your eyes all who place
their full trust in you will ultimately succeed according
to your plans.

Make a joyful noise unto God, all ye lands.

—*Psalm 66:1*

$\mathcal{I}$ should feel an overflowing of joy, shouldn't I, Lord? I know a believer should have a positive outlook, but that's hard for me right now. Joy is a struggle, especially with all that I've been through, but if you want me to be joyful, then please work a miracle in my life. Thank you for always listening to me.

$\mathcal{O}$n our way to rejoicing gladly let us go.
Christ our Lord has conquered; vanquished is the foe.
Christ without, our safety; Christ within, our joy;
who, if we be faithful, can our hope destroy?
On our way rejoicing; as we forward move,
hearken to our praises, O lest God of love!
Unto God the Father joyful songs we sing;
unto God the Savior thankful hearts we bring;
unto God the Spirit bow we and adore,
on our way rejoicing now and evermore.
On our way rejoicing; as we forward move,
hearken to our praises, O blest God of love!

—*John S. Monsell*

Chapter 11

. . . .

He that loveth not knoweth not God;
for God is love.

—*1 John 4:8*

*For we know that if our earthly house of this taber-
nacle were dissolved, we have a building of God, an
house not made with hands, eternal in the heavens.*

—*2 Corinthians 5:1*

God, so much of life is fleeting. It seems like we are
always saying goodbye to this person or that situation.
But there is one thing we can always count on—your
love. Like the foundation upon which our lives are built,
your love gives us stability, something to hold onto when
everything around us is whirling chaos. Like the roof
over our heads, your love shelters us from life's worst
storms. Thank you, God, for your everlasting love.

Nor height, nor depth, nor any other creature,
shall be able to separate us from the love of God,
which is in Christ Jesus our Lord.

—Romans 8:39

𝒥 find such comfort knowing that your love for me, Lord, knows no obstacles and can never be kept from me. Except for those obstacles I erect myself. I can be so foolish and stubborn sometimes, and do all kinds of things to block your love. I can try to control my own life, or the lives of my husband and

children. I can attempt to make things happen according to my will. But in the end, all of this blocks your love and your will for my life, and keeps my blessings from ever reaching me. Help me, Lord, to remove all blocks that stand between you and the everlasting love you promise.

And thou shalt love the Lord thy God with all thine heart, and with all thy soul, and with all thy might.

—Deuteronomy 6:5

𝒥 know yours is a persistent devotion, Lord. Your devoted love for me is the example that helps me to love others as well. What would I prefer to your love? What could I love more than those I hold dear? Nothing in the universe! Who are the loves of my life? Let me count them all and delight in them today.

I am the good shepherd: the good shepherd giveth his life for the sheep.

—John 10:11

𝑀y mother raised her children with so much sacrifice. She always put us first, so that we could have a better life than she had. Her parents did the same for her, and one day, as a mother, I will do so for my own children. Sacrifice is love in action, and nowhere is that action more important than loving, caring for, and protecting our children. God, I pray that I always give to my loved ones without concern for myself, knowing my reward will come from you. I pray that I may feel the generosity of spirit that comes when I offer my time, attention, and care to my family, without asking for anything in return. May I always be filled with more than enough love to go around.

Every good gift and every perfect gift is from above,
and cometh down from the Father of lights, with
whom is no variableness, neither shadow of turning.

—James 1:17

How good it is, Almighty One, to bask in the warmth of your love. To know nothing more is required than this: receive your good gifts from above.

Herein is my Father glorified, that ye bear much fruit;
so shall ye be my disciples.

—*John 15:8*

$\mathcal{L}$ord, how I pray that your love is evident in me today!
I want to follow you closely and help draw others to you
as well. I know that if those with whom I come in contact
see love, joy, peace, patience, kindness, goodness, faithfulness, gentleness, and self-control in me, they may find
you as well. Direct my steps as I follow you, Lord, and
may the grace you've sprinkled on me be revealed for
your glory. Amen.

For every creature of God is good, and nothing to be
refused, if it be received with thanksgiving:
For it is sanctified by the word of God and prayer.

—*1 Timothy 4:4–5*

$\mathcal{L}$ord, being in love is a magical gift. Everything seems
brighter and sharper in focus. My heart soars and my
spirit is light as air, and all because of the love of another.
But help me to also seek that deeper, more lasting love

that comes from truly knowing another, even when the fires of passion become a gentle and steady simmer. Let love always be in my life, no matter what form it comes in. Love of any kind is a magical gift. Thank you, Lord.

The word which God sent unto the children of Israel, preaching peace by Jesus Christ: (he is Lord of all).

—*Acts 10:36*

$\mathcal{L}$ove is an active force. When we "walk our talk" and live God's message of love, we create a community full of faith. When we do that, we are God's voice, his hands, and his light for each other. We are living love.

Withhold not thou thy tender mercies from me,
O Lord: let thy lovingkindness and thy
truth continually preserve me.

—Psalm 40:11

𝓔verything around me keeps changing, Lord. Nothing lasts. My relationships with others are different than they were before. I started to feel  as if there is nothing sure and steady on which I can depend. Then I remembered your ever-present, unchanging love. Through these transitions, your love gives me courage and hope for the future. Amen.

𝓘've seen the phrase "choose love" everywhere, yet I often find it hard to choose love when someone is making my life miserable, or my loved ones are hurting.

It becomes all too easy, God, to give into hate and anger, even when you are there to remind me of another way I can respond. I pray I always find my way back to love, no matter what the circumstances are around me. I pray you help me stay centered in love when I am about to venture into the territory of hatred or intolerance. Give me the strength and wisdom to always respond with love even when first instinct is to lash out and cause pain. There is always a choice, and I want to choose love.

If ye love me, keep my commandments.

—*John 14:15*

When we are young, we don't understand the importance of rules. We think rules were meant for someone else to follow. We break rules and don't think twice about the consequences, to ourselves and to others. As we get older and wiser, we realize rules are often there to assist us in making better decisions, and to guide and protect us. Lord, let me always live in accordance with your commandments, which you gave to show me the way to your kingdom. Help me to follow these rules of divine law, which keep me living in your will. May I always see the wisdom in following your Word, and may I always do so with love in my heart for you, Lord, for others, and for the world I live in.

As the apple tree among the trees of the wood, so is my beloved among the sons. I sat down under his shadow with great delight, and his fruit was sweet to my taste.

—*Song of Solomon 2:3*

𝒟ear God, I am lucky to have a soul mate. One must be strong and able to be happy alone, of course, but it's a profound comfort to have a partner with whom I can share joys and hardships. My husband and I have been together many years now, and we have grown together in love, trust, and tenacity. Being strong for one another has given us each courage. We support one another as individuals and together. And I enjoy his company! I feel lucky, Lord. My husband is a gift, and I praise you for this gift and blessing.

Whom having not seen, ye love; in whom,
though now ye see him not, yet believing,
ye rejoice with joy unspeakable and full of glory.

—1 Peter 1:8

 ather, thank you for initiating our wonderful relationship by loving me first! Your perfect love has taught me to trust you and leave my fear of your judgment behind. Your love for me brings such joy to my life, Lord. Help me spread this joy to others today.

But God commendeth his love toward us, in that,
while we were yet sinners, Christ died for us.

—Romans 5:8

 od, you proved your love by offering your son. What a sacrifice you made for me! I pray I can return that love in sacrifice to you. I ask that you guide me in service

and show me how I can be of help to you and to others.
Through your love, I ask to become a beacon of light
to guide others out of darkness. Show me how I can do
more to fulfill your will for my life. When I am of service,
God, I feel so whole and blessed and complete. May I do
your good works in the world, God. May I sacrifice for
you the way you sacrificed your son for me.

*But even the very hairs of your head are all
numbered. Fear not therefore: ye are of
more value than many sparrows.*

—*Luke 12:7*

*I*f God creates us in his image, he must value us. Then
why do so many people in the world today suffer from
loneliness, depression, and low self-worth? I myself have
struggled with low self-esteem, when I felt powerless and
unable to cope. But God made us in his image, and we
are worthy of all of his blessings and his love. He promised us this and he always keeps his word. God, help us to
recognize our inherent worth, and to realize that we are
loved. Help us know our value as your beloved children.

*There is no fear in love; but perfect love
casteth out fear: because fear hath torment.
He that feareth is not made perfect in love.*

—*1 John 4:18*

I cannot hold fear and love in my heart at the same time. When I am afraid, it crowds out every thought and emotion and I feel held hostage to it. That is when I need to turn to you, God, for the love that can cast out fear. Once I come back to your love, my heart begins to lighten and brighten, and my whole

perspective changes. What looked impossible to deal with, God, now becomes less intimidating. What held me captive in the grip of panic now loosens its hold and I feel free again. Thank you, God, for the perfect love that fills my heart when I come to you in times of fear, worry, and concern.

For thy mercy is great above the heavens:
and thy truth reacheth unto the clouds.

—Psalm 108:4

*H*is love is wider than our worries, longer than our loneliness, stronger than our sorrows, deeper than our doubts, and higher than our hostilities. This is why valleys are so wide, rivers so long, winds so strong, oceans so deep, and the sky is so high—with these, we can have a picture of the wonder of his love.

Let not mercy and truth forsake thee:
bind them about thy neck;
write them upon the table of thine heart.

—Proverbs 3:3

*F*aith in God's love frees me to be the real me, for I remember that God sees me as I am and loves me with all his heart.

And this is his commandment, That we should believe on the name of his Son Jesus Christ, and love one another, as he gave us commandment. And he that keepeth his commandments dwelleth in him, and he in him. And hereby we know that he abideth in us, by the Spirit which he hath given us.

—1 John 3:23–24

$\mathcal{L}$ove and faith go hand in hand. It is through faith in Christ that we're filled with his love, and it's his love flowing through us that shows our faith. That's why true love cannot operate outside of faith, and faith cannot be verified without the evidence of authentic love. Faith and love—the two go hand in hand.

*In this was manifested the love of God toward us,
because that God sent his only begotten Son into the
world, that we might live through him.*

—*1 John 4:9–10*

*L*ove isn't just a word; it's a verb, an action. Love falls flat when it is simply spoken, with no power behind it. God sent his son to manifest the word of his love into form and action, and we are blessed because of it. Now it is our turn to put our love into the world and spread the blessings. God, show us how we can become more loving. Show us how we can manifest miracles for each other, beyond just saying we believe in them. Show us how we can be love itself. Love isn't just a word. It is you, God, in action.

*Train up a child in the way he should go:
and when he is old, he will not depart from it.*

—*Proverbs 22:6*

Raising children is the hardest job there is. I often feel I come up short balancing love with being firm. I worry that everything I say or do will scar my children in some way. God, I ask that you guide me in my parenting and direct my ways so that my children benefit from my love and experience. I ask you to give me your amazing wisdom and grace so that I can set a good example. Help me as a mom to know the right things to do and say to raise my children into strong, loving, and caring adults, who will then love their own children the same way, as you, Father God, love us.

A new commandment I give unto you,
That ye love one another; as I have loved you,
that ye also love one another.

—John 13:34

Father in heaven, let me be an angel to someone today. Just as you have blessed my life with people who love and cherish me, let me be a light of love that shines upon someone who needs me. I have received the gift of angels, now allow me to give and be one in return.

Chapter 12

Praise and Thanksgiving

. . . .

By him therefore let us offer the sacrifice
of praise to God continually, that is, the
fruit of our lips giving thanks to his name.

—*Hebrews 13:15*

God made the beast of the earth after his kind,
and cattle after their kind, and every thing that
creepeth upon the earth after his kind:
and God saw that it was good.

—Genesis 1:25

God of all things, we thank you for all of your creatures, from the largest to the smallest. In each of these wondrous animals, we see your creative touch. Help us respect all you have created, to protect their lives, and to be ready to learn from them anything you would like to teach us.

Blessed be the Lord, who daily loadeth us with
benefits, even the God of our salvation.

—*Psalm 68:1*

*T*he house is a mess, Lord, and because of it, my attitude is a matching mood. Like handwriting on the wall of my grumpy heart, I got your message: 'Tis far wiser to hunt first crocuses on spring days than lost socks in the laundry; to sweep leaves into piles for jumping than grunge in a corner; to chase giggles rising from a child's soul like dandelion fluff than dust balls beneath beds. Bless, O Lord, this wonderful mess, and send me out to play.

The thief cometh not, but for to steal, and to kill,
and to destroy: I am come that they might have life,
and that they might have it more abundantly.

—*John 10:10*

*F*ather, this morning I woke up, and the gift of life was still within me. What a privilege! I don't want to lose wonder of it for even one day. Help me to live with purpose and joy, not waiting for what today might bring me, but rather looking for opportunities to be and do all that you've created me for. And, most of all, thank you for being with me in each moment, showing me the way of abundant living.

Continue in prayer, and watch in the same with thanksgiving.

—Colossians 4:2

*I*f I look hard enough, I find blessings in everything—even dirty dishes, unwashed laundry, and chocolate stains on the kitchen floor. Those things remind me that I am part of a family, and in our gratitude and thanksgiving we are part of God's family. Lord, give me watchful eyes to notice your love in the family chaos that surrounds me.

Blessed be his glorious name for ever:
and let the whole earth be filled with his glory;
Amen, and Amen.

—Psalm 72:19

$\mathcal{L}$ord, we praise you for all the beauty and wonder you've placed in the world. How creative of you to think of a creature as exuberant and joyful as the humming-bird! How interesting that you sprinkled spots on the backs of the newborn fawns that follow along behind their mother through our backyard. Let us never become so accustomed to your glorious creation that we take it for granted, Lord. You've blessed us with a wonderland, and we thank you for it.

Then were there brought unto him little children,
that he should put his hands on them, and pray:
and the disciples rebuked them.

—Matthew 19:13

O Lord, what a blessing children are in this world. They bring such joy into our lives and are a precious composite of the best of our past and the hopes for the future. Thank you for your love for all children, Lord. Please guard them always.

And now abideth faith, hope, charity, these three;
but the greatest of these is charity.

—1 Corinthians 13:13

I am infinitely blessed that in a world full of different people, you have chosen to give your heart to me. I am forever grateful that in a world full of different paths, you have chosen to walk beside me. I am eternally joyful that in a world full of different opportunities, you have chosen to create a life for me.

Enter into his gates with thanksgiving,
and into his courts with praise:
be thankful unto him, and bless his name.

—*Psalm 100:4*

$\mathcal{D}$ear God, you have blessed me with a loving, caring husband; wonderful kids; a beautiful home; friends I can depend on; and work that I love. We are all healthy and happy, and for that I give thanks. We are all blessed, but no one more than me. You have given me the gift of motherhood and of a family that means so much to me, and I will forever be thankful.

He that loveth his brother abideth in the light,
and there is none occasion of stumbling in him.

—*1 John 2:10*

$\mathcal{H}$eavenly Father, we are thankful for family. Please bring our family together in happiness. Help us see everything as your children do: with wonder and awe. Glorious are your creations! Thank you for creating us. We love our family. We love you. Amen.

A new heart also will I give you, and a new spirit will I put within you: and I will take away the stony heart out of your flesh, and I will give you an heart of flesh.

—*Ezekiel 36:26*

You fulfilled this promise, Lord, when you gave your Holy Spirit to live within those who dedicate their lives to you. Thank you for transforming my heart with your saving grace. You truly have brought my soul alive—as if from stone to living flesh.

I will praise thee; for I am fearfully and wonderfully made: marvellous are thy works; and that my soul knoweth right well.

—*Psalm 139:14*

Lord, each newborn baby is such a miracle. We marvel at the tiny hands and rosebud lips, and we know such a masterpiece could only come from you! We pray for all little children today, Lord. Watch over them and guide their parents. Grant all parents the courage, strength, and wisdom they need to fulfill their sacred duties.

Let every thing that hath breath praise the Lord. Praise ye the Lord.

—*Psalm 150:6*

God, help me celebrate this day with all my heart, to rejoice in the beauty of its light and warmth. May I give thanks for the air and grass and sidewalks. Help me feel grateful as others flow into my soul. May I cherish the chance to work and play, to think and speak—knowing this: All simple pleasures are opportunities for praise.

265

I will praise thee, O Lord, with my whole heart;
I will shew forth all thy marvellous works.

—*Psalm 9:1*

ℒord, I pray I will stop taking all your miraculous works for granted. Whether I praise you through song, words, or actions, I want to praise you not only for what you are doing, but also for all you have done in the past. Help me see the holiness of the ordinary in each day.

Being confident of this very thing,
that he which hath begun a good work in you
will perform it until the day of Jesus Christ.

—*Philippians 1:6*

Lord, help my eyes to see all the ways you are working in this world. Because of your great compassion, because of your active involvement, the effects of everything you accomplish are multiplied many times over. We praise you, Lord, and pray you will continue to be involved in our lives and in our world. And may our deeds and thoughts always honor you.

Let your light so shine before men,
that they may see your good works,
and glorify your Father which is in heaven.

—*Matthew 5:16*

Some prayers are best left unfinished, God of abundance, and this will be an ongoing conversation between us. Each day I discover new gifts you offer me, and the list of reasons to be thankful grows. As I accept your gifts and live with them thankfully, guide me to become a person who shares with others so that they, too, can live abundantly. May someone, somewhere, someday say of me, "I am thankful to have this person in my life."

But let all those that put their trust in thee rejoice: let
them ever shout for joy, because thou defendest them:
let them also that love thy name be joyful in thee.

—*Psalm 5:11*

Gracious Father, I have often asked myself this question: How do I make my home a place of joy? A place where my children and husband can relax and be happy? Now I know—the answer lies with you, O Lord. Our hearts are restless until they find their home in you. Joy begins when we let you in. Life seems steadier, brighter, friendlier, safer. Your presence fills us with music. We make joyful noises when we sing your praises. All thanks to you, precious Lord, for our happy home. I will sing to you as long as I live.

The Lord bless thee, and keep thee.

—*Numbers 6:24*

God, this morning my day started badly. My alarm didn't go off and I had to rush to get ready for work. It was raining and my hair was frizzy. My daughter has

a cold and she was grumpy at breakfast. As we raced around the house we snapped at one another about silly things: how I prepared the toast, the fact that she didn't clear the table when she was done eating. I felt lonely in my foul temper! And yet when I drove my daughter to school the sun came out, and I saw again how beautiful she is, with her clear bright profile and her keen mind, and when we parted she told me she loved me. God, help me to remember and appreciate all the blessings you have given me. Help me to remember what is truly important, and that in your love we are never alone.

Whereby are given unto us exceeding great and
precious promises: that by these ye might be
partakers of the divine nature, having escaped the
corruption that is in the world through lust.

—2 Peter 1:4

$\mathscr{E}$xceeding, great, precious. These words speak of overwhelming abundance, of profound importance, of something held dear. These are the words the Apostle Peter used to describe God's promises to us. And yet, do we take time to reflect upon and realize the treasures that they are? These promises! May we perceive their worth, and give God due thanks and praise for his goodness toward us.

And she conceived again, and bare a son:
and she said, Now will I praise the Lord:
therefore she called his name Judah; and left bearing.

—Genesis 29:35

$\mathscr{T}$he greatest miracles often occur right after the most barren of times. Have you noticed that? When I am

suffering and in pain, I remember that God promised to make all things right and restore what was lost. When I am depressed or afraid, I know God will lift the veil of illusion and show me I was loved and protected all along. I thank you, God, for never leaving me desolate or alone. I thank you for always bringing me out of the dark and into the light, and for rebirthing lost hopes and dreams in my heart, even when I thought all was lost from me forever. Thank you, God, for the restoration of my faith and my hope.

Who is like unto thee, O Lord, among the gods?
who is like thee, glorious in holiness,
fearful in praises, doing wonders?

—*Exodus 15:11*

Miracles come in all sizes and shapes. Sometimes they come in the form of other people. As a strong woman, I

rarely ask for help, thinking I can handle it all myself. But I can't. I've found that praying to God for help can result in a particular person calling or emailing with just the thing I need to get over a major hurdle. Or I run into someone at the store that has the answer I've been seeking to a nagging question. God's miracles are there if I keep my eyes open to see them! Thanks be to you, God, for never failing to send me your earthly angels to help me when I need it.

To the praise of the glory of his grace,
wherein he hath made us accepted in the beloved.

—*Ephesians 1:6*

Stop doing whatever it is you are doing right now and thank God, who makes all things possible. Put down the pen or the tablet, the cell phone or laptop, and turn off the TV. Take time to think about how his grace and love has filled every moment of your life, whether you were aware of it or not. Celebrate his loving presence and unfailing guidance. Do not take another breath without first thanking the God who is the breath of life itself. Stop for just a moment and say thanks to the one who created you in his image and provides you with every need.

Saying, I will declare thy name unto my brethren,
in the midst of the church will I sing praise unto thee.

—*Hebrews 2:12*

The last time I got praise from someone at work or at home, I felt like a million dollars. As a woman, I can honestly say being acknowledged means a lot, because we women can easily fall prey to doing too much for others and we get resentful, especially when it goes unnoticed. That is why I never fail to praise you, God, for all you have done with me and through me. I thank you, God, for being the reason for all the good seasons of my life. I sing your praises, God, to anyone who will listen and know the miracles of your grace. Just as I love to be appreciated, I know you do too, God, and I appreciate your constant loving presence each day of my life.

But ye are a chosen generation, a royal priesthood, an holy nation, a peculiar people; that ye should shew forth the praises of him who hath called you out of darkness into his marvellous light.

—*1 Peter 2:9*

So many people feel invisible and unloved. Think about your own life and ask if there is someone you've been ignoring or not appreciating. Too often, we think people don't need to hear how special and loved they are. Too often, we think others automatically know we cherish them. Today, I ask God to remind me as I go along to praise others and make them feel special. Not because I want to look good in God's eyes, but because they are special in my eyes, and they deserve to know. God, help me show my appreciation of others, especially those I sometimes forget about and take for granted.

I will worship toward thy holy temple, and praise thy
name for thy lovingkindness and for thy truth:
for thou hast magnified thy word above all thy name.

—Psalm 138:2

$\mathcal{I}$f I were to keep track, I would no doubt find that most of my prayers are complaints or requests. I feel guilty sometimes, wondering if God feels taken advantage of the way I do when people only come to me to whine or ask for something. God, I want to take time today to ask for nothing more than your time. I come to you in prayer today to say, "Thank you! Thank you!

Thank you!" Not just for the small miracles that fill my days, but for the challenges that build my character and resilience. Not just for the happy times, but the sad times, too. Thank you, God, for this life and everything in it. I am so blessed.

But I will hope continually,
and will yet praise thee more and more.

—Psalm 71:14

My old college friend Rachel is an artist. She lives in a city near my home, and occasionally she'll have a gallery showing of her work downtown. I always try to make her shows, and we usually also manage to get together for a meal every month or so. Her shows are a perfect time for me to compliment her work. But one evening when we were just meeting for dinner, I mentioned how impressed I am by a series of sculptures she's been making from pressed wood. Even though I had already praised that same work at a recent show, the innovative nature of the work has stayed with me, and I wanted to share that. Rachel was uplifted by my comment. It turns out she'd had a frustrating day in the studio and my admiration, coming from out of the blue like that, meant a lot to her. The experience reminded me that praise is not a one-time thing—you never know when another person might be struggling, or how much repeating a kind word can mean. God, may I remember to uplift others even as I praise you, again and again.

Let thy work appear unto thy servants, and thy glory unto their children. And let the beauty of the Lord our God be upon us: and establish thou the work of our hands upon us; yea, the work of our hands establish thou it.

—*Psalm 90:16–17*

When we give thanks and praise to someone, we honor the presence of God in that person. Our gratitude for the people we love is our acknowledgment of the Holy Spirit working through them.

*And when all the children of Israel saw how the fire
came down, and the glory of the Lord upon the house,
they bowed themselves with their faces to the ground
upon the pavement, and worshipped,
and praised the Lord, saying, For he is good;
for his mercy endureth for ever.*

—2 Chronicles 7:3

I can tell someone how great God is until I'm blue in the face, and they won't believe me. But when they see how happy I am, and how fulfilled and joyful my life is, they always want to know my secret. I tell them, "Get God!" Of course my life isn't always perfect. I have my bad times, too, but I am thankful that during those bad times, I have God to lean on and to guide me through. This is the gift of his glory I hope to share with others, not by my words, but by my life itself.

Therefore judge nothing before the time,
until the Lord come, who both will bring to
light the hidden things of darkness,
and will make manifest the counsels of the hearts:
and then shall every man have praise of God.

—1 Corinthians 4:5

$\mathscr{L}$ive and let live. It's a great mantra for being at peace with life. I know when I relax and give up playing God, things happen with ease and flow, just as he wills them. His presence gives me the wisdom to stop pushing and forcing and being a control freak. I am not in control anyway, so why not lighten up, let go, and let God? I pray, God, to be calm in mind and patient in spirit. I pray to end the madness and chaos of wanting to control everything, and let you be God instead. I thank you, God, for being the force behind my life.

Chapter 13

The Promise of His Presence

· ·

He discovereth deep things out of darkness, and bringeth out to light the shadow of death.

—Job 12:22

Teach us to know, God, that it is exactly at the point of our deepest despair that you are closest. For at those times we can finally admit we have wandered in the dark, without a clue. Yet you have been there with us all along. Thank you for your abiding presence.

And the Lord passed by before him, and proclaimed,
The Lord, The Lord God, merciful and gracious,
longsuffering, and abundant in goodness and truth.

—*Exodus 34:6*

Though each day I strive to be a positive role model and a loving mother, a wise and funny friend, daughter, or spouse, I do not always live up to my potential. I am not always as patient as I could be. I am not always as clear-sighted or kind. Thank you, Lord, for always being there with me—even on days when I am not at my best—and for your patience with my faults. Thank you for seeing the good in me and helping me to realize it. Please guide me as I try to be the best person I can be; please help me to persevere even on the most difficult days, to remember that when I fail, you are always there to raise me up. Sustained by you, may I meet each day with an open heart and gracious spirit.

For thou art great, and doest wondrous things:
thou art God alone.

—*Psalm 86:10*

$\mathcal{M}$y Creator, blessed is your presence. For you and you alone give me power to walk through dark valleys into the light again. You and you alone give me hope when there seems no end to my suffering. You and you alone give me peace when the noise of my life overwhelms me. I ask that you give this same power, hope, and peace to all who know discouragement, that they, too, may be emboldened and renewed by your everlasting love.

For thou art my lamp, O Lord:
and the Lord will lighten my darkness.

—*2 Samuel 22:29*

$\mathcal{H}$eavenly Father, I ask for your bright presence. When I leave you behind and try to go about my day without your guidance, Lord, it's like groping around in the dark. I stub my heart on relational issues. I trip over my ego. I bump into walls of frustration. I fall down the steps of my foolish choices. How

much better to seek the light of your presence first thing and enjoy the benefit of having you illuminate each step of my day!

But know that the Lord hath set apart him
that is godly for himself: the Lord will hear
when I call unto him.

—*Psalm 4:3*

With so much praying going on in the world, I wonder if God really hears my prayers. The psalmist had no doubt: "Know that the Lord hath set apart him that is

godly for himself: the Lord will hear when I call unto him" (Psalm 4:3). It's a comfort to know that the God of the universe is not too busy or distracted to attentively bend his ear toward me. God is listening and is present in my life.

*Teaching them to observe all things whatsoever I have
commanded you: and, lo, I am with you always,
even unto the end of the world.*

—*Matthew 28:20*

$\mathcal{T}$he Bible promises that God will always be with us. Whether we are commuting to work, having coffee with friends, taking a walk, or even sleeping soundly through the night—whatever it is, wherever we are, he's there with us. He's the friend who always has time, never moves to another part of the world, is forever ready to listen, and provides the best counsel. It's just a matter of realizing he's there. The Gospel of Matthew closes with this powerful promise: "I am with you always, even unto the end of the world."

*Thou wilt shew me the path of life:
in thy presence is fulness of joy;
at thy right hand there are pleasures for evermore.*

—*Psalm 16:11*

There is joy in being in God's presence. There's no other place we find joy in its fullness, shimmering in all its facets, except in the presence of God himself. We can try manufacturing our own versions of joy by pursuing some of life's temporary pleasures—achievements, recreation, entertainment, material possessions, and such. But these don't come close to the rarified joy we experience when we draw close to our heavenly Father so we can spend time in his presence.

Let your conversation be without covetousness;
and be content with such things as ye have: for he
hath said, I will never leave thee, nor forsake thee.

—*Hebrews 13:5*

Anyone who has ever been abandoned deeply fears that they will be abandoned again. Often the worm of insecurity eats away at subsequent relationships, weakening and eventually destroying them. This, in turn, feeds the existing fear. It's a cycle of destruction that has no cure in human relationships, for even if our loved ones are faithful, still they are mortal. That's why God's promise to never leave or forsake us is such a powerful assurance. When we lay hold of it even with a seed of faith, over time God's unfailing presence causes our seedling faith to grow up into an unshakable oak of security.

Father, how I need the security of your presence! You are truly the only one who can say that you will never abandon me. For you will be with me always: in life, in death, and in the life to come.

Be strong and of a good courage; be not afraid,
neither be thou dismayed: for the Lord thy God is
with thee whithersoever thou goest.

—Joshua 1:9

ℒord, what a relief it is to know that whether I'm going
to the corner grocery for milk and eggs or on a multicity
adventure via planes, trains, and automobiles, you are
with me. You never have a scheduling conflict, and you
are more necessary than my car keys or boarding pass.
Thanks for always coming along, Lord. Some days
I could hardly take a step outside my house without
leaning on you.

And David was afraid of the Lord that day, and said,
"How shall the ark of the Lord come to me?"

—*2 Samuel 6:9*

God, I made a mess of things today. I meant well: I leapt out of bed with a smile. But as the day progressed, I found myself losing composure. It was a long commute, and when someone cut me off I felt my temper rising. A meeting ran late and I had to change a lunch appointment. My friend expressed disappointment and at that point in the day, knee-  deep in work, I felt too stressed to listen and respond with grace. Where was the calm, gracious person I was determined to be only this morning? And yet through it all, I know you love me and are with me. Thank you for always blessing me with your loving-kindness. Thank you for reminding me that, with you, there is always another chance to be my best self.

Rejoice evermore. Pray without ceasing.
In every thing give thanks: for this is the will of God
in Christ Jesus concerning you.

—*1 Thessalonians 5:16–18*

God, the blessed feeling of being at home in your loving presence is like nothing else. The joy I feel when I know I never walk alone is the greatest of gifts, and when I look around at the wonderful people you have chosen to walk with me through life—my family and my friends—I truly know that I am loved. Thank you, God, for these miracles, these blessings, far too numerous to count. And to think I never have to look too far from home to find them is the best miracle of all.

Let us come before his presence with thanksgiving,
and make a joyful noise unto him with psalms.

—*Psalm 95:2*

Lord, how blessed we are to be able to see you all around us and to sense your presence within us. Even though we can't see you in the same way we might see a friend or a neighbor, we see you in your Word and in all that is good and true in the world around us. Thank you, Lord, for making yourself so available to us.

Jesus again unto them, saying, I am the light of the world: he that followeth me shall not walk in darkness, but shall have the light of life.

—John 8:12

There's a path straddling the Montana-Idaho border— an old railroad bed that's been converted into a "rail trail" for bicycles. This fifteen-mile stretch is touted as "one of the most breathtaking scenic stretches of railroad in the country," with seven high spans and ten tunnels. One of these tunnels stretches for nearly two miles. Without a bicycle light, it would be virtually impossible to ride through without falling or crashing. A lightless rider's best hope would be to find another rider with a light and ride very close to that individual. Life, too, is beautiful in places, but it can also be treacherous. The best way to make it through is by staying close to Jesus, the light of the world.

Who can find a virtuous woman?
For her price is far above rubies.

—*Proverbs 31:10*

What is virtue? To me, God, it is keeping a strong moral compass and adhering to a code of goodness despite the complexities of modern life. Life can be unfair. It can be cruel. We each have, every day, myriad excuses for not taking the high road—for exacting revenge, indulging in gossip, for harboring anger or hatred within our hearts. Lord, help me to feel your presence and to stay the course. Help my children and loved ones to navigate the world with grace and compassion. May hardship never dull our sense of what is virtuous and correct, and may we meet our days with energy, joy, and a renewed sense of what it means to put grace into the world.

Hear my voice, O God, in my prayer:
preserve my life from fear of the enemy.

—*Psalm 64:1*

God, keep me close today. I am not at my best, and I would like someone to listen as I whine, moan, and complain. Please bear the brunt of my troubles or send someone to help in your name. Amen.

There shall not any man be able to stand before thee
all the days of thy life: as I was with Moses, so I will
be with thee: I will not fail thee, nor forsake thee.

—*Joshua 1:5*

Thank you, God, for never failing me in good times or bad. In my life I have encountered all manner of people: lifelong friends, false friends, family who comforted me in my cradle and then stood beside me as I grew. But life brings change again and again. Death takes our loved ones; fair-weather relationships fade in the face of adversity or with time; children grow and leave our homes to make their own rich lives. These changes can be difficult—sad, disappointing, or even scary. I sometimes fear change and the loss it can bring. And yet, I don't need to fear what is still to come because you have promised to stand with me all the days of my life. You have promised not to fail or forsake me. I come to you today to be renewed by your presence and your promises.

For by grace are ye saved through faith;
and that not of yourselves: it is the gift of God.

—*Ephesians 2:8*

As a busy, working woman, I spend a lot of time doing things for other people. When I get home from work, I spend more time doing things for my family. Sometimes I feel empty and depleted, drained and taken for granted. God, you never fail to find some small saving grace to fill me up again. You never stop loving me or guiding me or showing me that even amidst a busy, crazy life, there are miracles brewing. In you I find peace amidst the chaos, and calm among the storms. In you I come home to rest and take comfort after a long, difficult day. Thank you, God, for the grace of your presence in my life.

Heal me, O Lord, and I shall be healed; save me,
and I shall be saved: for thou art my praise.

—*Jeremiah 17:14*

There is nothing the Lord won't do for me when I simply turn to him in praise. I have bad things happen just like anyone else, but his presence lifts my burdens and lightens my load. I turn to the Lord for healing of my body, mind, and spirit, knowing he will not deny me. I pray, dear Lord, to always walk in your presence. I pray you will forever be by my side as I journey through life's peaks and valleys. I pray, Lord, for the comfort and joy of knowing you will save me from my enemies and forgive me my sins. I can depend on you, Lord, to always have my back, even when those I count on have abandoned me.

He is the Rock, his work is perfect:
for all his ways are judgment: a God of truth and
without iniquity, just and right is he.

—Deuteronomy 32:4

If everyone stopped judging others, the world would be a much more compassionate place. The media is full of examples of people ripping each other apart over differences of opinions and beliefs. It only creates division and intolerance, and the world has enough of that as it is. God, you alone are the judge and you alone are right in all your ways. This is the rock of truth. Help us all to stop pushing our own personal brand of justice and righteousness upon each other. Help us recognize that we are all a part of the perfection of your plan and not each other's enemies. God, watch over us and lead us to a more loving way of being in the world.

But the Comforter, which is the Holy Ghost,
whom the Father will send in my name, he shall teach
you all things, and bring all things to your
remembrance, whatsoever I have said unto you.

—John 14:26

Why is it so hard to be kind? It's as if people don't want to take the time to show compassion to others. Are we that distracted by our gadgets that we cannot share a word or two with another human being face to face? Are

we so busy we cannot be of comfort to someone hurting? God, I vow to always be kind when I can, and to offer a helping hand and a caring heart to others in your name. I ask that you work with me and through me to spread the spirit of your presence wherever I may go. I pray, God, to be a light unto the world as you would have me be.

And it shall come to pass, that whosoever shall call on the name of the Lord shall be saved.

—*Acts 2:21*

God promises we will have a joyous, prosperous life if we do nothing more than call upon him. That's it! We don't have to suffer for his love and miracles. We just have to be willing to invite his presence into our hearts and our homes and we can be transformed. This is such a powerful and profound truth, and yet how many times do we try to live of our own will and force life to be what we think it should be? How often does that work out? God, I pray you will always be the biggest part of my life, and that your presence will always guide me. I pray that the bond we share grow stronger with time and that my faith and trust in you will be rewarded.

And it shall come to pass afterward,
that I will pour out my spirit upon all flesh.

—Joel 2:28

After Jesus' ascension, his disciples did as he had instructed and waited prayerfully for the promise. At Pentecost, ten days after Jesus had left them (promising he would return one day), the Spirit was poured out in an unmistakable way. The promise of God's presence with us by his Spirit is a gift that remains with us today. All who belong to Christ have the identifying mark or seal of God's Spirit working in their lives and are called daily to follow is direction and leading.

Or despisest thou the riches of his goodness and forbearance and longsuffering; not knowing that the goodness of God leadeth thee to repentance?

—*Romans 2:4*

No matter how badly someone has sinned, the promise of God's love is enough to make them repent. I've seen this happen many times with people I never thought would change. But one experience of God's presence, and they did change, becoming renewed and reborn in spirit. God can do that. God can take what is dark in us and turn it to light. I pray, dear God, that you help those who most need it, and find those who are lost and alone. Lead them to the promise of your grace and mercy, and heal what is broken in them. The world is often a scary place. I pray, God, that you work your miracles in many hearts today.

Peter said unto them, Repent, and be baptized every one of you in the name of Jesus Christ for the remission of sins, and ye shall receive the gift of the Holy Ghost. For the promise is unto you, and to your children, and to all that are afar off, even as many as the Lord our God shall call.

—*Acts 2:38–39*

I don't like to admit when I am wrong. I think a lot of my female friends can relate! I try to be wise and mature for my kids, and helpful to my spouse and friends, but sometimes I fall short and am just plain mistaken. That's when I must set aside my pride and ask God to help me make things right, even if that means going against my own desires. Life is about compromise, and learning as we go and grow. I thank God for rewarding my humility with his loving presence. I thank God for gifting me with his wisdom and guidance, even when it means admitting I was wrong.

Whither shall I go from thy spirit? or whither shall
I flee from thy presence? If I ascend up into heaven,
thou art there: if I make my bed in hell, behold,
thou art there. If I take the wings of the morning,
and dwell in the uttermost parts of the sea;
Even there shall thy hand lead me,
and thy right hand shall hold me.

—Psalm 139:7–10

$\mathcal{T}$he threat "You can run but you can't hide" gets
turned on its head in this passage—transformed into a
promise of God's presence with us in all places. The Lord
will never be left behind when we're in a place that seems
distant or unfamiliar. In fact, he's already there. It's a great
promise to keep in mind whether we're headed to the
dentist today or on a trip around the world.

The kingdom of God is not meat and drink; but righteousness, and peace, and joy in the Holy Ghost.

—Romans 14:17

I work overtime to provide the best home I can for my family. I want the best for my children and that often means material things like clothing and school supplies. I am doing my best to teach them how to earn and save money on their own, but more importantly, I am teaching them to first work towards being happy and kind and to live in the spirit of God's will. I want to be an example for them of a person who knows the promises of God are more than just physical and material, but also of the spirit and soul. I pray, dear God, to be a guiding light for those aspiring to experience your unseen blessings and miracles.

Chapter 14

Serving Others

. . . .

**And in every work that he began in the
service of the house of God, and in the law,
and in the commandments, to seek his God,
he did it with all his heart, and prospered.**

—2 Chronicles 31:21

The angels do your work, Father. I want
to do it, too. You made me a person, not
an angel. I can't fly through time or travel
the universe, but I am willing to do whatever I can. Help me see your agenda and
stick to the plan.

*And the King shall answer and say unto them, Verily I
say unto you, Inasmuch as ye have done it unto one of
the least of these my brethren, ye have done it unto me.*

—*Matthew 25:40*

*H*eavenly Father, when you sent Jesus, you gave your
best to us. As I consider how to go about emulating that
kind of love, I'd like to give in a significant way to someone
who is in need. There are many, many opportunities to
give, but I'd like to do more than just buy a gift; I'd like
to give myself.

*For though I be free from all men, yet have I made
myself servant unto all, that I might gain the more.*

—*1 Corinthians 9:19*

*L*ord, my God, your son took on the role of a servant
to all people. As a mother, I try to walk in his footsteps.
Service to my family has become life's greatest pleasure. I
give myself willingly, not because someone demands that I
serve, but because I want to.

As I cook and provide meals, wash clothes, and maintain my home as a place of comfort for my family, my heart sings with the joy of fulfillment. When I consider that no job was too lowly for Jesus, even scrubbing the floor brings me satisfaction.

I thank and praise you, Father, for turning an independent person like me into a willing servant in your kingdom.

Serve the Lord with gladness:
come before his presence with singing.

—Psalm 100:2

Serving is one of the reasons we are on this earth and the reason Jesus himself said he came to the earth. When we serve, we reach out to meet the needs of others; service is an outward sign that we belong to God and desire to do his will. True service is not about grudgingly doing for others because of obligation, but an act that flows willingly, as a channel for God's love. True servants give not just with their hands, but also with their hearts.

My little children, let us not love in word,
neither in tongue; but in deed and in truth.

—*1 John 3:18*

$\mathscr{I}$ wish to extend my love, Lord. So give me hands quick to work on behalf of the weak. Make my feet move swiftly in aid of the needy. Let my mouth speak words of encouragement and new life. And give my heart an ever-deepening joy through it all.

Lord, thou hast heard the desire of the humble:
thou wilt prepare their heart, thou wilt cause thine
ear to hear: To judge the fatherless and the oppressed,
that the man of the earth may no more oppress.

—*Psalm 10:17–18*

$\mathscr{I}$f we look to service for the benefits it will bring us, we may be disappointed. Yet, if we forget about the benefits and gladly serve others, good things happen to us. We are helped in so many ways by those we serve.

And he said to them all,
"If any man will come after me, let him deny himself,
and take up his cross daily, and follow me."

—*Luke 9:23*

I had a cute poster in my childhood room that read, "It's hard to be good." All these years later, I still remember the message! I didn't want to take my mom to the doctor last week, and would rather have stayed home to paint. Much to my son's chagrin, I counseled him to honor a commitment he'd made to a friend even though a "better" invitation came along. God, service comes at a price; it can feel inconvenient or painful. Help me follow you even when doing so seems difficult or inconvenient.

If we are devoted to the cause of humanity, we shall soon be crushed and broken-hearted, for we shall often meet with more ingratitude from men than we would from a dog; but if our motive is love to God, no ingratitude can hinder us from serving our fellow men.

—*Oswald Chambers*

For ye have need of patience, that, after ye have done the will of God, ye might receive the promise.

—*Hebrews 10:36*

O God, you have called each of us to special tasks, purposes, and vocations, equipping us with the skills and energy to perform them. For some, our vocations send us into the labor force. For some, it is soon bringing retirement. For some, it is in full-time homemaking. For some, our vocations are in artistic skills. For some, in volunteering, helping, and neighboring. Always, there is that first call from you, God of vision, working through us to help, heal, and change a needful world.

One of the principle rules of religion is to lose no occasion of serving God. And since he is invisible to our eyes, we are to serve him in our neighbor, which he receives as if done to himself in person, standing visibly before us.

—*John Wesley*

Blessed are the poor in spirit:
for theirs is the kingdom of heaven.

—*Matthew 5:3*

Remind us, Lord, that you dwell among the lowliest of people. You are the God of the poor, walking with beggars, making your home with the sick and the unemployed. Keep us mindful always that no matter how much we have, our great calling is to depend on you—for everything, every day of our lives.

I will pray the Father, and he shall give you another
Comforter, that he may abide with you for ever.

—*John 14:16*

*D*ear heavenly Father, today, if I see or hear of someone who is struggling in some way, please help me take a moment to remember what it was like when I was struggling and you helped me through the aid of a friend or stranger. Let that memory mobilize me to offer help and be your true servant. Amen.

He that oppresseth the poor reproacheth his Maker:
but he that honoureth him hath mercy on the poor.

—*Proverbs 14:31*

I long to help every needy person in the world, Lord. Perhaps the most effective way to do this is by praying that you will send help wherever it is needed. Meanwhile, there is my corner of the universe with its many needs, and some of these are surely within my reach: half of my sandwich to the person standing near the freeway ramp with a sign; an evening spent going through my closet and setting aside items to donate; a weekend afternoon of helping with events at my church; a monthly visit to the sick, homebound, or imprisoned. It's a privilege to honor you by extending your compassion—in person.

For the oppression of the poor, for the sighing of the needy, now will I arise, saith the Lord; I will set him in safety from him that puffeth at him.

—*Psalm 12:5*

God, I look around my community today and I feel helpless. The homeless, the hurting, the needs each one represents are more than I can handle. But you can do it. You can meet each need. Teach me. Strengthen me and use me to serve as I reach out to a neighbor or a stranger and meet just one need at a time!

Being filled with the fruits of righteousness, which are by Jesus Christ, unto the glory and praise of God.

—*Philippians 1:11*

ℒord, please help me to remember that you are the source of all good things that come out of my life as I grow and flourish in you. All the "good fruit" of love, joy, peace, patience, kindness, goodness, faithfulness, gentleness, and self-control come directly from you and then produce good things in me. I want to thank you for nourishing and supporting my life. Please use the fruit you're producing in me to nourish others and lead them to you as well.

But the manifestation of the Spirit
is given to every man to profit withal.

—1 Corinthians 12:7

God, make me an open vessel through which the waters of your Spirit flow freely. Let your love move through me and out into my world, touching everyone I come in contact with. Express your joy through the special talents you have given me, so that others may come to know your presence in their own lives by witnessing your presence in mine. Amen.

Now therefore so shalt thou say unto my servant
David, thus saith the Lord of hosts,
I took thee from the sheepcote, from following the
sheep, to be ruler over my people, over Israel.

—2 Samuel 7:8

Lord, I have many roles in life. I am by turns a wife, a mother, a daughter, a sister, a friend, and an employee. Some of my roles are informed by caregiving and it is an honor and a privilege to take care. Yet society does not always give as much attention or respect to those who care for others. Not necessarily glamorous, caregiving can be an "invisible job": significant but not acknowledged in terms of the energy, love, and skill entailed. Lord, thank you for recognizing that each role I play matters. Thank you for reminding me that when I care for another, I am living Christ's teachings. You take the most humble among us and lift them up in your glory.

Behold, we count them happy which endure.
Ye have heard of the patience of Job,
and have seen the end of the Lord;
that the Lord is very pitiful, and of tender mercy.

—James 5:11

Over and over I ask myself, "What can I do?" What can I do to make a difference? One of the hardest things about reaching out is having others think I can "fix it"

and then finding out that I can't. Lord, help me to remember that what you promise is not to "fix it" for us, but rather to give us whatever it takes to prevail in spite of our hurts. Help me keep in mind that sometimes all that is necessary is a listening ear.

But thou, O Lord, art a God full of compassion,
and gracious, long suffering,
and plenteous in mercy and truth.

—Psalm 86:15

It is easy to be judgmental. It is easy to write another person off when they fall short of our expectations. Even those we love will disappoint us. Yesterday I was short with my sister when she called to let me know that she won't be able to take our mother shopping this weekend. I was counting on her help, and at first, I wouldn't let myself hear her explanation: Her own daughter is sick, and her husband, my brother-in-law, has been pulling extra shifts at work. It took effort for me to overcome my own annoyance and listen to what she had to say. Dear Lord, help me to remember that compassion comes from you.

May I be inspired by the compassion you show me every day, and may I in turn show compassion to others.

Now therefore ye are no more strangers and foreigners, but fellow citizens with the saints, and of the household of God.

—*Ephesians 2:19*

$\mathscr{I}$n my house, things usually work best for everyone when we all pitch in and work together. In the house of God, we must be of service to one another in the same spirit. We may be strangers in one sense, but in another we are interconnected and we share a fellowship around our love of God and our desire to do his will. Let us all learn to work together in service to the whole, because when the whole is happy, every individual benefits. God, help us to think not just of ourselves and our own needs, but the needs of our families, our communities, and our planet.

And we know that all things
work together for good to them that love God,
to them who are the called according to his purpose.

—*Romans 8:28*

I can make myself crazy wondering what my purpose is for being alive. I come up with all kinds of explanations and reasons, like being a great mom or wife, or being a supportive friend, or excelling at my career. The truth is, these are the human roles I choose to play, because my true purpose is to love God, and to spread the power of his love to everyone I meet. Above any other purpose for my existence, this alone gives me fulfillment. God, when I am living on purpose, the rest of my life falls into place with ease and grace. God, I pray to always live in accordance to your will.

She stretcheth out her hand to the poor;
yea, she reacheth forth her hands to the needy.

—*Proverbs 31:20*

ℐ am shocked by the treatment of the poor and needy in this country. Even people who claim to love God shun the poor and treat them as if they are less than human. It breaks my heart because God taught us to love everyone, including those less fortunate, and to reach out a helping hand to those in need. These are his ways, and so few live by them. God, I pray I never give in to greed and intolerance. I pray I always have an open and loving heart towards those who are struggling, no matter the reason for their struggle. That is not my place to judge. All you ask of me, God, is that I love others as you love me. May I always be generous and giving to all of your beloved children.

Let no corrupt communication proceed out of your
mouth, but that which is good to the use of edifying,
that it may minister grace unto the hearers.

—*Ephesians 4:29*

$\mathcal{G}$od, help me speak positive and empowering words to myself and to others. I know the power words can have to build or break down, to create or destroy. May I always use words to lift up and create, especially

with my children. I know from experience how unkind things can stay stuck in the brain forever, causing low self-esteem, depression, and lack of self-worth. I know that something said years ago can still punish and hurt today. God, let me be a vessel of goodness, kindness, and compassion. And when I forget to choose my words carefully, I ask that you stop me, God, and let me choose words that show love.

Greater love hath no man than this,
that a man lay down his life for his friends.

—John 15:13

Few of us will ever be asked to sacrifice our lives for our friends. But we are often asked to sacrifice time and energy when they need our love and support. Yes, we all lead busy lives and sometimes we just want to be left alone, but a friend in need should never be ignored, because one day, we might be the friend in need. Would we not hope our friends would be there for us? God, remind me to always leave some room in my day and some love in my heart for kind words, a supportive ear, and a shoulder to lean on. Let me always be there for those I love, no matter how tired or burdened my own life feels.

I have shewed you all things, how that so
labouring ye ought to support the weak,
and to remember the words of the Lord Jesus,
how he said, It is more blessed to give than to receive.

—*Acts 20:35*

Lord, you have blessed me with so much in my life. I enjoy giving to others and seeing the smiles on their faces. It makes me happy and in a way, I receive just as much as I give. But lately I've been feeling like I don't give enough. I've been caught up in my own little life dramas and I've not been as generous and charitable. Open my heart again, Lord, to the joys of sharing with others. I feel so closed off, Lord. Help me find that spirit of compassion and freedom that comes from helping others and not just focusing on my own problems.

As every man hath received the gift,
even so minister the same one to another,
as good stewards of the manifold grace of God.

—*1 Peter 4:10*

*T*oday I received a letter from a woman I am sponsoring in Rwanda through a Christian charity. It filled me with such joy and renewed my spirit. In the eight months I have been sponsoring her, I haven't bothered to write her a single letter. Receiving this letter prompted me to take the time to finally write to her. When I stopped to think about her situation, I also thought of my own life circumstances. Lord, I am a much-blessed woman and it's my duty as a Christian to pass on the gifts I have generously been given. Remind me that giving is about more than a monthly charge on my credit card. Let this connection with a woman less fortunate than me serve as a reminder of how much I gain by giving to others.

For bodily exercise profiteth little: but godliness is profitable unto all things, having promise of the life that now is, and of that which is to come.

—*1 Timothy 4:8*

We live in a society that is so focused on the physical body. We run, walk, exercise, and go to the gym, comparing our bodies to others. We diet and "watch our figures." We become so obsessed with our bodies, we forget the importance of keeping our minds and spirits in shape. But God promises us an amazing life when we stay focused on his presence. He even promises us a life beyond this one. God, I pray for a sound body, mind, and spirit. I pray for a strong and resilient body and a powerful spirit to serve you with. I know my own self-worth is developed as I help and serve others.

Thou shalt not hate thy brother in thine heart:
thou shalt in any wise rebuke thy neighbour,
and not suffer sin upon him.

—Leviticus 19:17–18

It is tough to admit I have the ability to hate someone. Hatred is such a strong word, and such a sinful energy, but there are evil people I hear about on the news that provoke such powerful feelings of anger in me. People who hurt children and animals, or abuse their partners. The world can bring out the hate in me if I let it. But God asks that I instead keep my heart free of judgment and condemnation. God asks that I keep my own house in order before demanding that another do the same. I ask, God, that you always keep me from hating and judging others. It only serves to hurt me, and keep me blocked from your blessings.

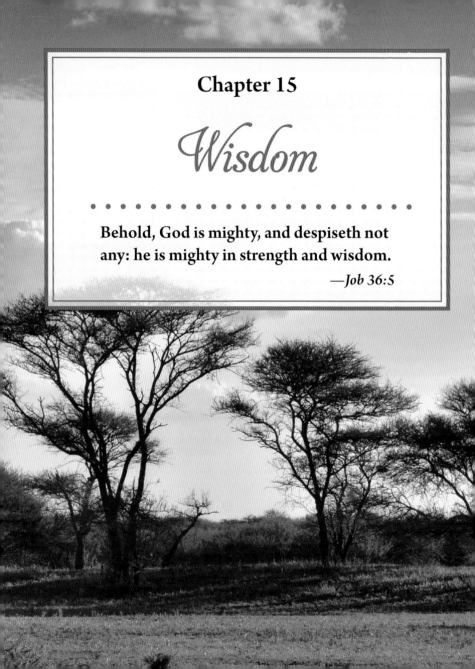

Chapter 15

Wisdom

Behold, God is mighty, and despiseth not
any: he is mighty in strength and wisdom.

—*Job 36:5*

If any of you lack wisdom, let him ask of God,
that giveth to all men liberally, and upbraideth not;
and it shall be given him.

—James 1:5

God, you promise to give wisdom to anyone who asks for it. This offer has only one condition: that we ask in faith, not doubting your promise. Well, since you're offering, I'm not going to be shy about asking. I need wisdom. I need it today as I'm dealing with people and situations and wondering what the best approach or decision might be. Thank you for being generous with your gifts rather than giving them to only a select few. In fact, you make receiving them as simple as just asking. You never cease to amaze me with your generosity, Lord. I'm deeply grateful for your promise of wisdom.

Who is wise, and he shall understand these things?
prudent, and he shall know them? for the ways of the
Lord are right, and the just shall walk in them:
but the transgressors shall fall therein.

—Hosea 14:9

$\mathcal{I}$ am here right now, Father, because I do want to walk in your ways. I know the key is staying connected to you because the ways of the world are all around me, always imposing a different set of values and a different worldview. Give me a wise and discerning heart in all things today so I can stay on track.

My brethren, count it all joy when ye
fall into divers temptations; Knowing this,
that the trying of your faith worketh patience.

—James 1:2–3

$\mathcal{G}$od, I give thanks for the wisdom you share with me when I am trying to understand my own actions or someone else's. You know what is best, and you have my highest good in mind. I will turn to you for the advice and guidance I need. Thank you, God, for being a strong and loving presence in my life. Amen.

Every word of God is pure:
He is a shield unto them that put their trust in him.
—*Proverbs 30:5*

$\mathcal{I}$ have a friend who has read the Bible from cover to cover, and she described it as a profound experience. I have not read the Bible in this manner; I have favorite verses but, truth be told, the biblical prose can be intimidating. I do not always understand how the verses apply to my broken dishwasher or sick pet. And there are so many interpretations, sometimes conflicting, of what is within the Bible's pages! God, grant me a clear, level head and an open heart so that I might understand the wise ways of your Word. May the rich stories, the adventures and drama, and instruction that the Bible has to offer, be accessible to me. May I have the wisdom to apply its contents to my day-to-day life, and may I always be open to your teachings.

For wisdom is a defence, and money is a defence:
but the excellency of knowledge is that
wisdom giveth life to them that have it.

—*Ecclesiastes 7:12*

$\mathcal{S}$o many people have their heads in the sand about the problems and issues of our world. To me, knowledge and wisdom are priceless, especially the wisdom you, God, provide me to act with love and integrity in all my affairs. With your will in my heart, I trust not only will I have the strength to face my own issues, but those of the greater good. When I am out of your will, I am no good to anyone. I ask, God, that you always keep my focus on being a part of the solution, not the problem, because the world doesn't need more problems. Life is a gift for those wise enough to understand we are all in it together.

There is no wisdom nor understanding
nor counsel against the Lord.

—*Proverbs 21:30*

When I was young, I thought I knew it all. Yet my life was a mess and it finally occurred to me that maybe I didn't know as much as I claimed to. Oh, the arrogance of youth. But over the years I have come to rely on your wisdom, God, and not my own, and the wonderful miracles in my life are a testament to that. If I rely only on myself and my own stubborn will, things don't work too well. If I rely on your counsel, God, they usually go pretty smoothly. If I act on my own, things get messier. If I act with you at my side, miracles occur. Thank you, God, for helping me to see I am nothing without you!

Even a fool, when he holdeth his peace,
is counted wise: and he that shutteth his lips is
esteemed a man of understanding.

—Proverbs 17:28

There is a time for speaking up, and a time for shutting up. Grant me the wisdom to always know the difference. My husband and kids say I talk too much, and I admit it has gotten me into hot water more than a few times, especially in arguments with family and people I work with. It is hard to stay quiet when someone presses your buttons and you want to react and respond, but it usually makes things worse.

I ask, Lord, that you give me the wisdom to know when it is best to talk about a problem and offer a solution, and when to hang back and stay silent, not sticking my nose, or my voice, in other people's business.

But the wisdom that is from above is first pure,
then peaceable, gentle, and easy to be intreated,
full of mercy and good fruits,
without partiality, and without hypocrisy.

—James 3:17

*W*hen I read this verse, I realize how perfectly Jesus personified heavenly wisdom. It's a wonder to me that we are called to walk in his footsteps, but then I remember that it is only possible to do it through the Spirit that works in and through us. Thank you, Lord, for making the things of heaven available to those who seek them.

Through wisdom is an house builded;
and by understanding it is established:
And by knowledge shall the chambers be filled
with all precious and pleasant riches.

—Proverbs 24:3–4

*T*hank you for your wise ways, Lord. Following them fills my life with true blessings—the riches of love and relationship, joy and provision, peace and protection.

I remember reading in your Word that whenever I ask for your wisdom from a faith-filled heart, you will give it, no holds barred. So I'll ask once again today for your insight and understanding as I build using your blueprints.

But we speak the wisdom of God in a mystery, even the hidden wisdom, which God ordained before the world unto our glory.

—1 Corinthians 2:7

God, I have such a limited perspective of the world. I have limited wisdom of how I should act in that world. Many times, when I've been unsure of what to do, you put an idea into my mind I never would have thought of, or gently nudge me to consider a solution I didn't even know existed.

Your ways are such a mystery, yet I know that you know all and see all and therefore can help me live in a manner that goes far beyond the confines of my small view and often smaller expectations. Thank you, God, for always urging me to think higher, act higher, and live higher.

Behold, I have done according to thy words:
lo, I have given thee a wise and an understanding
heart; so that there was none like thee before thee,
neither after thee shall any arise like unto thee.

—*1 Kings 3:12*

God, thank you for giving me a kind heart and a wise mind. There was a time when my friends didn't want to spend much time with me because I was always too busy doling out advice and not simply being a loving friend. I thought I was helping, but was instead being annoying. I understood over time a real friend offers unconditional love before giving any advice, no matter how wise the advice. My friends noticed the change in me, and I noticed a new depth to my relationships. Love and wisdom go together, and those who have both, shine.

*For the commandment is a lamp; and the law is
light; and reproofs of instruction are the way of life.*

—Proverbs 6:23

ℒord, your Word is so alive—so vibrant—that it almost
seems illuminated when I am reading it. When I am
troubled, opening the Bible is like turning on a com-
forting light in a dark, gloomy room. Thank you, Lord,
for loving us so much that you gave us your wisdom to
illuminate our lives.

Call unto me, and I will answer thee, and show thee
great and mighty things, which thou knowest not.

—*Jeremiah 33:3*

God, we know that pain has produced some wisdom in our lives, but it has also created cynicism and fear. People turn on us, reject us, hurt us, and none of us wants to play the fool more than once, so we're tempted to close off our hearts to people and to you. But relationships that bring meaning require vulnerability. Help us trust you to be our truest friend and to lead us to the kind of community that will bring healing, not destruction.

Wisdom is the principal thing; therefore get wisdom:
and with all thy getting get understanding.

—*Proverbs 4:7*

Not a day goes by when I don't do something without thinking, and regret it instantly. With all the distractions of life, I often act without first checking in with you and asking to discern your will and your wisdom. And I pay the price for my ignorance and impatience when my problems

get bigger, not smaller. But I am learning, Lord, and with each passing day I am stopping more often to ask for your wisdom for whatever situation or challenge I'm facing. I've found that wisdom trumps quick knee-jerk reactions every time. Thank you, Lord, for helping me understand it's okay to slow down, do the right thing, and have no regrets later.

He is like a man which built an house,
and digged deep, and laid the foundation on a rock:
and when the flood arose, the stream beat vehemently
upon that house, and could not shake it:
for it was founded upon a rock.

—Luke 6:48

*G*od, help me to build on a firm foundation by relying on your wisdom, diligently seeking your direction in all I do, and learning to walk in your paths of kindness, peace, and justice to my fellowman.

God gave Solomon wisdom and understanding
exceeding much, and largeness of heart,
even as the sand that is on the sea shore.

—1 Kings 4:29

I don't have a lot of money, God, so when I think about giving to others, I often feel as though I have nothing of value to offer. Then I remember the times I sat with my grandparents before they passed away, listening to their stories and experiences, absorbing their wisdom, and cherishing their advice. I realized I have so much to offer to those around me. I have love and life experience and enough wisdom to help those who ask for it. I have a heart full of compassion and understanding. I have kindness. Thank you, God, for the gifts you instilled in me so I could pass them on to others...gifts no amount of money can buy.

Martha was cumbered about much serving,
and came to him, and said, Lord, dost thou not care
that my sister hath left me to serve alone? bid her
therefore that she help me. And Jesus answered and
said unto her, Martha, Martha, thou art careful and
troubled about many things: But one thing is needful:
and Mary hath chosen that good part, which
shall not be taken away from her.

—*Luke 10:40–42*

$\mathcal{I}$ have Martha days and I have Mary days, Lord. Some days lend themselves to a worshipful response more than others. But Mary didn't let everyday tasks distract her from an opportunity to glean wisdom from you. Help me carve out time each day to be attentive to your Spirit. My to-do list will always be there on the back burner.

The glory of young men is their strength:
and the beauty of old men is the grey head.

—*Proverbs 20:29*

ℒord, time and again I see that you intend for the generations to go through life together. The joy the youngest child brings to the eldest grandparent is such a blessing to all who witness it. Even when it isn't possible for us all to be together all the time, let us see the wisdom in sharing our lives. Please keep us ever alert to the unique gifts each generation has to share.

*Blessed is the man that walketh not in the counsel
of the ungodly, nor standeth in the way of sinners,
nor sitteth in the seat of the scornful. But his
delight is in the law of the Lord, and in his
law doth he meditate day and night.*

—*Psalm 1:1–2*

My friends and I gossip. We like to give advice, too, even if we don't follow it ourselves. When I am with my friends, it is all too easy, Lord, to slip into these roles and find myself saying and doing things that aren't in accordance with your will. I fall back into human ways, and then wonder why I feel out of balance. Help me to remember that life works best when I stay in alignment with your thoughts, Lord, asking myself throughout the day, "Is this my will at work here, or yours?"

With the ancient is wisdom; and in length of days understanding. With him is wisdom and strength, he hath counsel and understanding.

—*Job 12:12–13*

*M*y parents died when I was a young woman, barely out of school, and at first, I proceeded through life almost blindly. I made my way as best I could, but sometimes it was a lonely road. I have learned in the years since that God puts people into my path, to help guide me, and when I remain open, I can benefit from the knowledge others have to share. Many of these folks are older than me. They possess the wisdom born of experience, and a broad worldview that helps me to keep perspective. Dear Lord, please may I always remember to seek instruction from those who have gone down the path before me.

$\mathcal{H}$onoring our parents is wise. In Ephesians 6:2–3, Paul wrote, "Honour thy father and mother; which is the first commandment with promise; That it may be well with thee, and thou mayest live long on the earth." That's a weighty and wonderful promise! Even in adulthood, we can find ways to honor those who raised us. It's gratifying—even if there's a difficult situation—to rise above the difficulty and let God's love prevail.

$\mathcal{S}$eeking wisdom is wise. It may sound like a redundancy, but it's not. The quest for wisdom is wise in itself—a worthy pursuit no matter how old or young we may be. The writer of Proverbs exults: "Happy is the man that findeth wisdom, and the man that getteth understanding. She is more precious than rubies" (3:13, 15). Finding wisdom means that we need to look for it, and that in itself is wise.

Chapter 16

Bessed are the peacemakers: for they shall be called the children of God.

—Matthew 5:9

When the circumstances of my life feel like a storm is blowing through—uprooting, flooding, twisting, burying—I can feel myself getting frantic, Father. I want to be able to do something to stop it, but I am powerless to change the course of something so beyond my control. And it's only when I stop flailing and grasping like a drowning swimmer that I realize you are holding me, that you have not left me to brave the elements on my own. Whatever may be damaged, lost, or destroyed is also in your hands, and you are the one who restores, heals, and redeems, if only I will give you time to show me.

And he said to the woman,
Thy faith hath saved thee; go in peace.

—Luke 7:50

Heavenly Father, let me carry your peace inside me today and use it as an anchor against the tumult of my daily life. It's so easy to get lost in my routines and my to-do lists. The day's demands threaten to blow me off-course, but the knowledge of your strength and omnipotence can serve as a touch point, bringing me back to serenity again and again. Help me remember that whatever my outward circumstances, peace is only a heartbeat away. Amen.

These things I have spoken unto you,
that in me ye might have peace. In the world
ye shall have tribulation: but be of good cheer;
I have overcome the world.

—*John 16:33*

$\mathscr{L}$ord, we stand on your promises, but when it comes to your promise that your peace is with us, we sometimes stand confused. Where is your peace when young soldiers are killed in war? Where is your peace in the middle of the night when a sick child cannot be comforted? Where is your peace when a marriage is irretrievably broken? Yet even when we cannot see your peace, Lord, we know it is there because of your promise. We can find it in these and all circumstances when we come to you humbly and ask you for it. Thank you for your unfailing promise of peace. Amen.

He that dwelleth in the secret place of the most
High shall abide under the shadow of the Almighty.

—*Psalm 91:1*

*S*preading your great branches
Over all who come,
Sheltering humble hearts
From judgment's burning sun.
Here your shade of mercy
Stirs breezes deep within.
In heaven's center planted
We find you once again.

$\mathcal{G}$od wants us to know peace is in every area of our lives—peace in our daily work, our business, our family, and our soul. The key to letting peace enter in is to invite God into each of these areas daily.

The Lord will give strength unto his people;
the Lord will bless his people with peace.

—*Psalm 29:11*

$\mathcal{W}$hen a woman of faith has a sense of knowing who she is and what she is about, her inner peace and beauty are like a brilliant light, drawing people to the truth and love she lives in.

And the peace of God, which passeth all understanding,
shall keep your hearts and minds through Christ Jesus.

—*Philippians 4:7*

*D*ear God, I long to feel the peace you bring, the peace that passes all understanding. Fill my entire being with the light of your love, your grace, and your everlasting mercy. Be the soft place that I might fall upon to find the rest and renewal I seek. Amen.

*L*ord, I know I should be feeling your peace right now, but it's just not happening. I need for you to examine my motives, my ambitions, my feelings and fears. Show me how this lack of peace is my own doing, because I know it is. Help me to get out of my own way, Lord, so I can return to the peaceful place you desire for my soul. Thank you in advance for answering my cry for peace. I love you, Lord. Amen.

*L*ord, is peace possible when my life is filled with activities, responsibilities, and worries? I wish I had time to sit and just be with you—listening for your quiet voice amidst the tumult. Instead, I am caught up in the everyday, and I fear I'm moving farther from you. Please show me the way back to you, to your Word and your will for me. I know that the only way to find you is to seek you, and that you will always find me. Amen.

Thou wilt keep him in perfect peace, whose mind is stayed on thee: because he trusteth in thee.

—*Isaiah 26:3*

*P*eace comes to those who know it is an inward state of mind, not an outward state of being. When we've attained inner balance and harmony, nothing that occurs outside of us can disrupt that claim. Those who have true peace of mind know that they can meet both good fortune and misfortune with a positive attitude and achieve an equally positive outcome. Inner peace depends not on outer circumstance, but on how we choose to react to it within.

$\mathscr{H}$eavenly Father, accept my thanksgiving for the wonderful life you have given me. My family is healthy, my work is fulfilling, and I feel a deep sense of peace inside that I have not felt for a long time. I am so grateful to you for continuously prov-

ing to me that your will is always better than mine and that your point of view is much bigger and broader than the narrow perceptions of my little life. I live each day in gratitude knowing that there is peace in my life when I look beyond the surface of things to where you are, always present: always there. Amen.

Ask, and it shall be given you; seek, and ye shall find;
knock, and it shall be opened unto you: For every one
that asketh receiveth; and he that seeketh findeth;
and to him that knocketh it shall be opened.

—*Matthew 7:7–8*

$\mathcal{L}$ord, in the midst of the least peaceful situation imaginable, I want to reflect your peace. I ask you to open my heart so that I can feel your peace in the midst of chaos and confusion. And once I find it, Lord, please use your holy power to enable your peace to shine through me into the lives of others. I want to be a reflection of the kind of calm and peace that can only come from you. Use me, Lord. In the midst of chaos, use me.

For to be carnally minded is death;
but to be spiritually minded is life and peace.

—*Romans 8:6*

$\mathcal{H}$eavenly Father, thank you for the centeredness you bring to my life. Even when every external thing is in an uproar, I can still come back to that still, small place and feel your Holy Spirit. I know you are with me always and that I am your beloved. I can rest in your presence in complete peace, knowing you will protect and shelter me. Thank you for your never-failing love. Amen.

He caused an east wind to blow in the heaven:
and by his power he brought in the south wind.

$\mathcal{A}$ll around leaves are falling, drifting, swooping in
the wind. They become a whirligig, a dance of wind
and nature. They are a picture of the heavenly places
where lighthearted beings are carried by the invisible
power of your love.

$\mathcal{T}$he raging storm may round us beat,
A shelter in the time of storm;
We'll never leave our safe retreat,
A shelter in the time of storm.
Oh, Jesus is a Rock in a weary land,
A weary land, a weary land;
Oh, Jesus is a rock in a weary land,
A shelter in the time of storm.

—Vernon J. Charlesworth

$\mathcal{L}$ord Jesus, your peace is so far from me today. I feel
separated, with all my calm leaking from the broken places.
I have no patience, even for those whom I love the most.
Please lay your hand upon me, lending me some of your

strength and stillness, so I may pass it on to others in my life. Heal my worry, still my unrest, so that I may be filled only with thoughts of your goodness and peace. Amen.

Depart from evil, and do good; seek peace, and pursue it.

—*Psalm 34:14*

ℬless me with a peacemaker's kind heart and a builder's sturdy hand, Lord, for these are mean-spirited, litigious times when we tear down with words and weapons first and ask questions later. Help me take every opportunity to compliment, praise, and applaud as I rebuild peace.

$\mathcal{G}$od, when all else fails, I know that I can count on you to give me rest and help me find peace. I am grateful to know that no matter what is going on in my life, I have someone who understands and who I can lean on. Sometimes

I forget, and I lash out in anger or frustration at those I love, but you forever remind me that I only need to go within and find a place where mercy and love and peace await, and my anger and frustration disappears. Thanks be to you, God.

$\mathcal{L}$ord, help me quiet the noise of life long enough to find in that sacred silence a peace that knows no end. With all the clutter of daily life, I need all the solitude I can get to renew and refresh my spirit after a long, busy day. Your peace is the center I can return to time and again, a place I can rest and let the concerns and worries melt away. Guide me to this place of peace within now. Amen.

$\mathscr{D}$ear Lord, some people are like stormy weather that can cloud up fair skies in a hurry. Just the sight of them entering a room can make me wish I could crawl into a cave until the storm of their words and ways passes by. I don't like feeling this way about anyone. I don't want to hide. I want to be like a warm sunshine set in a bright blue sky that either wins them over or chases them away just by virtue of it being what it is. I pray that your Spirit of love, joy, peace, patience, kindness, goodness, faithfulness, gentleness, and self-control would be just that in my life, and that your peace would prevail in each "human storm" that comes my way.

$\mathscr{L}$ord Jesus, I so want to walk in your footsteps, being a beacon of love, light, and hope for this broken world. I long to fulfill your plan for me, to grow into the path you have set out for me. Let me share the secret of my inner peace

with all who see me by acting as you would act and loving as you would love, each and every day. Amen.

Behold, I will bring it health and cure, and I will cure them, and will reveal unto them the abundance of peace and truth.

$\mathcal{M}$ental illness can be so devastating and stigmatizing, Lord. Few understand the heartaches involved in diseases that carry no apparent physical scars. Be with those friends, neighbors, and family members who deal daily with difficult situations of which we are often unaware. Touch them with your special love, and let them know that they can lean on you, Lord. Ease their burdens, quell their sadness, and calm their desperation. Bring peace and healing to these households. Remind them of the promise of your everlasting love.

$\mathcal{W}$e look forward to the time when the power to love will replace the love of power. Then will our world know the blessings of peace.

—William E. Gladstone

And he said, Draw not nigh hither:
put off thy shoes from off thy feet, for the place
whereon thou standest is holy ground.

—*Exodus 3:5*

Help us to relax, Lord of calming seas, so that we don't become numb to the joy and awe of children, of family. For it's socially acceptable to kick off our shoes and tangibly feel the love. Make us alive, O God, to the holy grounds of life, and save us from taking these special places for granted.

Lord, how often in our search for peace do we forget to simply follow your gentle guidelines? You tell us to forgive others. If we do, we will have peace. You tell us to love our enemies. If we do, we will have peace. You tell us not to worry about what we will wear or what we will eat, but to take comfort by considering the lilies of the field and the birds of the air. If we do, we will have peace. You tell us not to worry so much about storing up stuff, but to store up treasures in heaven! If we do, we will have peace. Thank you, Lord, for showing us the way. Keep our feet on the path to peace you planned for us. Amen.

𝒪 Lord God, who has given us the night for rest, I pray that in my sleep my soul may remain awake to you, steadfastly adhering to your love. As I lay aside my cares to relax and relieve my mind, may I not forget your infinite and unresting care for me. And in this way, let my conscience be at peace, so that when I rise tomorrow, I am refreshed in body, mind and soul.

—*John Calvin*

$\mathcal{D}$ear Father, your quiet is so large that no sound can upset it. Your peace is so deep that no earthly worry can disturb it. You hold all the chaos of this world within you, and still you are completely calm. You are eternal and endless, and nothing I can do or say will ever upset you, forever and always the God of peace. Knowing that you are eternal and everlasting, unending and merciful gives me comfort in my powerlessness, for you are good and just. Amen.

Wherefore, my beloved brethren, let every man be swift to hear, slow to speak, slow to wrath: For the wrath of man worketh not the righteousness of God.

—James 1:19–20

$\mathcal{L}$ord, I feel angry with so many people. Often I think my life would be peaceful if only they would just do the right thing. I convince myself they are robbing me of peace, but at this moment I know it's my choice to let go of anger and embrace peace. Staying angry with them for not living up to my expectations doesn't solve any problems—it just creates new ones. Please help me to remember that anger doesn't bring about the righteous life that God desires—in me or in those I'm staying angry at. Give me strength to release them—over and over again if need be—so I can go back to that serene, tranquil place called "peace." In Jesus' name, amen.

*H*eavenly Father, it is good to remember that everything that lives and breathes is sacred to you. We must never feel superior to any other human being—for we are all precious in your eyes. You have given us life, and we must make the choices that lead to kindness and peace. You created us, but how we live together is up to us. Thank you.

*S*urely there is something in the unruffled calm of nature that overawes our little anxieties and doubts: the sight of the deep-blue sky, and the clustering stars above, seem to impart a quiet to the mind.

—*Jonathan Edwards*

I can do all things through
Christ which strengtheneth me.

—Philippians 4:13

ℒord, I am overwhelmed with the whirl of activity around me. Getting the children up and dressed, making breakfast, taking them to school, doing dishes, cleaning house, running errands, fielding phone calls, meeting appointments, retrieving the kids, supervising homework, delivering them to music lessons and sports practices, dealing with calamities...how do I fit it all in? I am buckling under the weight of each day, only to find that I must get up and start all over again the next.

Father, you are a God of peace and tranquility. I long to find a time to sit down and talk to you. Show me a quiet place in the midst of the frenzy, where I may commune with you, be refreshed, and know that through your strength, I can accomplish all that you have set out for me to do today.

The words of wise men are heard in quiet more than the cry of him that ruleth among fools.

—*Ecclesiastes 9:17*

The world is a noisy place. From family to office to leisure and routes in between, the air vibrates with ear-grabbing, relentless chatter. I yearn for quiet conversations with the God of still, small voices. My spirit, like my body, is easily bruised by too much noise. Help me hear you, God. Help me shut out the world when you talk.

Holy God, may your peace visit our household. May you be with us when we rise, helping us set our schedules for the day. May you be with us each minute as we go through our routines. May you be with us as we sit down to eat together,

and may you be with us as we lay down to sleep at night. May each member of our family acknowledge your presence, feel your loving hand, and rest in your peace. Amen.

Peace I leave with you, my peace I give unto you:
not as the world giveth, give I unto you.
Let not your heart be troubled, neither let it be afraid.

—John 14:27

I admit that the slightest distraction can pull my mind out of its orbit around you, Father. You know how I am: I can be praying or praising you one minute, and the next moment a phone call with some disturbing news or a careless driver cuts me off and POOF!—my peace has left the building, and I'm all out of sorts. I want to ask you, though, to help me. I want to grow into a more steadfast frame of mind—one that can take bad news and thoughtless people in stride, acknowledging them for what they are, but not allowing them to rattle my world. Would you help me take a step in that direction today? Thank you, Father.

*F*ather in heaven, sometimes I feel anger welling up inside me, and I need to turn to you for counsel. Please stay near to me and help me to find ways to express my emotions without harming another's feelings or getting myself so upset I cannot see past my own feelings. I need to understand myself, express myself, and accept myself—all within the bounds of your teachings. Amen.

The Lord will give strength unto his people;
the Lord will bless his people with peace.

—*Psalm 29:11*

ℋeavenly Father, our diversions seem great. We can't remember when the insurmountable demands started piling up, and we have a hard time seeing the end. Allow us to take a moment from our hectic days to close our eyes and feel your peace. We ask you to lead us. Amen.

ℒord, you are teaching me that finding peace requires me to seek it out—to look for and pursue peaceful places, peaceful ways, and peaceful relationships. If I make living in peace a priority, I won't miss it, and even when storms come my way, I will know where to find rest and

calm and quietude of spirit. Your Word so often pairs righteousness and peace. To live uprightly is to live in peace. Help me, Lord, choose what is right and true and good today, as I seek to live in your peace.

I celebrate today the peace of God within, a peace that is with me through the hours and never lets me down. God, your peace is my cornerstone, upon which I build the foundation of my life. In your peace, I spread peace to my family and friends, and to my community, for this indeed is a world that needs more peace. Blessed am I to have found that peace in you, God.

For unto us a child is born, unto us a son is given:
and the government shall be upon his shoulder: and his
name shall be called Wonderful, Counsellor, The mighty
God, The everlasting Father, The Prince of Peace.

—Isaiah 9:6

Almighty God, how blessed we are that when you chose to send your son to this earth it was not as the prince of power and domination, but as the Prince of Peace. You knew we would need his peace both as nations populating the earth together and in the innermost places of our hearts. Hear our voices lifted up in gratitude, O God! We are a people who could not survive without the Prince of Peace in our lives. Thank you for your indescribable gift.

Jesus said, "Blessed are the peacemakers: for they shall be called the children of God" (Matthew 5:9). It seems that there's a peacemaker in every family—the mom or dad, sister or brother who tries really hard to move everyone toward a peaceful resolution when conflict arises. To seek the path of peace is a reflection of God's own heart of reconciliation. When our children or protégés emulate us in good ways, we say joyfully, "That's my girl!" or "That's my boy!" Similarly, God is delighted to call us his children when we seek the path of peace.

You calmed the stormy waters, dear God, and quieted the thunderous skies. I ask you to calm the stormy waters for me as I struggle with the challenges I face. I know that with the peace you provide, I can face any obstacle and get through any trial or tribulation before me. In the stillness within, you wait for me, always present, always ready to bring me safely back home as a lighthouse guides a ship through the cold, dark fog to the comfort of the shore. Thank you for calming my storms, God.

$\mathcal{G}$od's Spirit produces peace. Peace begins in our hearts. If we lack peace within, we'll be hard-pressed to find a situation or circumstance that doesn't feel frustrating or unsettling. It's good to know, then, that we can experience and enjoy inner peace as we walk with God's Spirit, for "the fruit of the Spirit is . . . peace" (Galatians 5:22). Paul also urged, "Let the peace of God rule in your hearts, to the which also ye are called in one body" (Colossians 3:15). Such a call reveals God's kind intentions toward us as his Spirit leads us along.

$\mathcal{P}$raise the Lord! I am on the path of righteousness, and I will not stray. Nothing can separate me from you, for nothing else brings me the deep tranquility of the soul that I crave, nothing except your guiding love. You are my alpha and my omega, and I am complete in you. With your power, I can handle all of life's difficulties and problems, for with you all things are possible. I am at peace in your love. Amen.

*R*enounce all strength, but strength divine,
And peace shall be for ever thine.

—William Cowper

*C*reator God, what an amusing creature you made when you created the duck! As relaxing as it may be to watch him glide across the surface of a glassy, still pond on a summer's evening, we know he's paddling madly under the surface of the  water. He's also always looking for little fish or bugs to eat, and while we're entertained when he puts his head under water and waves his tail in the air, he's really diving for survival! Is that how you see us? Calm on the surface, but paddling madly underneath—with the occasional dive for survival? All your creatures need your constant provision and care, O God. Calm our ruffled feathers, and give us your peace. Amen.

$\mathcal{F}$ather, I am at war with myself over so many things. I would like to call a truce and find peace inside. Help me to see that all is not black and white, right and wrong, and that sometimes just taking a different perspective is all that is needed to stop the battle within. I long to understand the peace that you promise, and to cast it out into my world as a light that goes before me, making smooth my path. Father, help me to lay down my arms and find peace within. Amen.

$\mathcal{O}$ Lord, how amazing that just a small amount of peace, when carefully tended, can turn into pure contentment and joy. Today, Lord, make me aware of places I can plant seeds of peace into the lives of others. Could it be as simple as a gentle reply to a statement made in anger or making time to sit and listen to a troubled friend when I'd rather go home? Show me these opportunities, Lord. For I know that if I plant even the smallest seed of peace, you can nurture it to create a more peaceful world. To you be the glory! Amen.

$\mathcal{W}$here there is peace, God is.

—*George Herbert*

$\mathcal{D}$ear God, have mercy on me. I have been living my life lately with so much anger and hostility, so much frustration and irritation. Help me to find that calm center within; where your presence offers the peace I seek. Help me to take that peace and bring it out into my home, my community, and my world and to treat others as I would have them treat me. I need to be at peace, for only when I am peaceful within can I hope to create a peaceful place for others who share my world with me. Have mercy on me, God, and teach me to be at peace today.

$\mathcal{L}$ord, we hear so much about the quest for world peace on the news today. Politicians, journalists, and even pastors call for peace as if it were an option the world can provide. But we know that true peace can only come from you, Lord. And so we ask that you send your unique, powerful peace into the heart of every battle that is raging—those we can see, and those that are yet to be revealed. You are the only source of lasting peace, Lord. Please bring it to our world.

*F*ive enemies of peace inhabit with us—avarice, ambition, envy, anger, and pride; if these were to be banished, we should infallibly enjoy perpetual peace.

—*Petrarch*

*H*oly God, be with me today. I am entering a battle-field, and I am girding myself with your armor. I have a war against evil to fight, and though the enemy is strong, I know that righteousness will prevail. I go forth in complete peace, knowing that you are in control, that I am in your care, and have nothing to fear. I need no other protection than you, for you are with me today, tomorrow, and always. Amen.

$\mathcal{I}$ sing out in praise today, for the Lord has made me whole. My life is filled with peace and balance, and harmony is the order of my day. My life was not always like this. I once took on way more than I should have, and it wore me down. But in God's love, I now stand restored and at peace with whatever each new day brings. I know in my heart that I can handle anything as long as I am connected to the source that is my God. It is a source from which I can find all the highest and best blessings life has to offer. It is a source of pure peace.

*I will both lay me down in peace, and sleep:
for thou, Lord, only makest me dwell in safety.*

—*Psalm 4:8*

Quietly, calmly, Lord, you move in my life. Unseen, yet always present, your love is a powerful force I can rely on when I feel alone and unsettled. Swiftly, surely, Lord, you work for my good. Always you have my best interests in mind, and your timing is always the perfect timing for that goodness to show up in my life. Strongly, securely I rest in your profound peace, a place I can always go to when I need to get away from the noise and the bustle. Sweetly, gently you remind me each night when I lay down to sleep, that you are watching over me, and all is well in my world.

First keep the peace within yourself, then you can also bring peace to others.

—*Thomas à Kempis*

*H*eavenly Father, please bring peace to the relationships in my life. Some of the toughest challenges I have as a Christian involve my relationships with others. Even though we are brothers and sisters in Christ, we struggle to love each other and to treat each other with patience and loving-kindness. Today, please bless me with an extra dose of inner calm, that I might retain my composure and remember your laws as I am dealing with others. I long to do what is right, and I know that with your help, I can keep your commandment to love others. I ask in your son's name, amen.

*D*ear God,
Drop thy still dews of quietness,
Till all our strivings cease;
Take from our souls the strain and stress,
And let our ordered lives confess
Thy beauty of thy peace.

—*John Greenleaf Whittier*

*G*od, bring peace to the rough places in the world. Bring hope to the hearts that have grown cold and love to the souls that know only violence and despair. Bring wisdom and understanding to those who see around them only chaos. Bring comfort to those who suffer. For you alone can show this world what true and lasting peace is, the peace that is available to us all if we lay down our prejudices and our pride and take up instead love and tolerance. God, bring peace to the dark places of the world, that they may know light.

*H*eavenly Father, be with those who need you today. So many in this world have never felt the peace that passes understanding, the calm and serenity that comes when we turn over our lives to your wise and loving guidance. Instead, they live their lives alone, not realizing you are only an arm's reach from them. For each struggling soul, I pray that you would offer them your boundless mercy and love, helping them to come to know you.

$\mathscr{B}$efore prayer
I weave a silence on my lips,
I weave a silence into my mind,
I weave a silence within my heart.
I close my ears to distractions,
I close my eyes to attentions,
I close my heart to temptations.
Calm me O Lord as you stilled the storm,
Still me O Lord, keep me from harm.
Let all the tumult within me cease,
Enfold me Lord in your peace.

—Celtic Traditional

$\mathscr{M}$y own failures, foibles, and flaws are like storms of shame and frustration that recur regularly in my life, Lord. That's why I want to learn to look at them from your perspective. How do you see those things? It seems as though they tether me to you, reminding me of my need for your grace and mercy and love. They keep me from wandering too far away from you in an arrogance-fueled self-assurance. They remind me to be gentle with others who are struggling. They are opportunities to grow. They nurture the peaceful quality of humility in my life. Next time I stumble, Lord, remind me of these things. Keep me from letting unnecessary storms ruin the day you have made for me to rejoice in.

$\mathcal{I}$ can picture the satellite hurricane pictures, Father. They show a huge swirling pattern of dangerous weather. But right in the center, there is an eye—a place of perfect peace. If a person could remain in that eye, even though there are deadly winds blowing all around them, they could ride out the storm unharmed. To me, Father, the world is the like one of those storms, and you are like the eye. Please hold me, carry me, keep me where your peace remains at all times, no matter what is going on in the world around me.

$\mathcal{S}$ometimes I begin to slip into the illusion that I am in control of my world, Father. I imagine that I can arrange things just the way I like them and that I can create my own peace by making sure everyone and every-thing follows my plan. Oh, how that house of cards gets blown away in the winds of adversity! How quickly I am reminded that I cannot  manufacture peace with manipulation. You are my peace. You are my source of well-being, safety, and security. Apart from you there is no true peace to be had.

When a man's ways please the Lord,
he maketh even his enemies to be at peace with him.

—*Proverbs 16:7*

Father, I've noticed that when I make my primary objective to treat people with kindness and respect (instead of focusing on our differences of beliefs, values, or opinions), there is a level of respect I receive in return. Even people who might be religious or political "enemies," so to speak, are inclined to permit me my perspectives without being antagonistic toward me. It's even true sometimes that zealous would-be opponents treat me favorably, not because I water down what I believe in, but because your love can have that effect on people. And when your love touches our lives, it subdues animosity and fosters peace. Thank you for showing me how good your command is to love my neighbor as myself. By treating others as I would want to be treated, I can bring some much needed peace into this world.